Insider's Guide
TO **CAREERS IN URBAN PLANNING**

Foreword by **RICHARD FLORIDA**
by Planetizen Editors Tim Halbur and Nate Berg

Published by **PLANETIZEN** PRESS

Insider's Guide to Careers in Urban Planning

© 2009 by Urban Insight, Inc.

Published in the United States by Planetizen Press (www.planetizen.com), an imprint of Urban Insight, Inc.

Editors: Tim Halbur and Nate Berg
Foreward by: Richard Florida
Book design: Mindy Oliver

ISBN: 978-0-9789329-4-7
Library of Congress Control Number: 2009941613

First Edition

PLANETIZEN PRESS

PLANETIZEN *is an online resource for news and information, with daily news stories, features, job listings and opinion pieces exploring the world of city planning. You can find us at www.planetizen.com.*

Cover photos (clockwise from top): ® Opticos; courtesy of Sound Transit; courtesy of the City of Raleigh

Table of Contents

Foreword

by Richard Florida

I have two degrees in urban planning – a PhD from Columbia and a BA from Rutgers in political science and urban planning. I've found it to be a great career, because it's afforded me a great deal of flexibility. I'm interested in lots of things, so urban planning suited me. But that's not the only reason I chose it. I figured if I couldn't get a job in academia, or if one day those jobs dried up, urban planning gave me much better odds at getting a job in the real world than a degree in, say, political science or history. For my money, urban planning is the best field to be in if you have broad interests and have a zest for big concepts that can be grounded in real-world practice.

I've taught in public policy programs and now in a business school, so I am familiar with those programs as well as urban planning. Yet I find myself recommending urban planning to lots and lots of young people and students. I think it's because it is such a broad field. You get to learn about geography and economics and sociology, and also about land use planning, urban design and architecture, even geographic information systems. Some say the MFA is the new MBA. I say urban planning is among the very best ways to prepare yourself for the future.

Urban planning now encompasses such a variety of jobs that any array of temperaments and skill sets should be able to find a gratifying fit. Planning is a field that depends—even thrives—on strategic collaboration and cooperation, which means a range of different strengths and personalities are needed. Designers who come up with wildly inventive blueprints for using public space still rely on the quiet, diligent community board lobbyist to get their plans built. Before great ideas can be translated into concrete realities, the expert

Richard Florida

negotiator is as important as the visionary or the traffic engineer. Whatever career you choose, you will not be bored—or lack the opportunity to wrestle with the most pressing issues of our time.

Place is the key element of our ever-expanding global economy. The way I see it, our cities and communities are well on their way to replacing the industrial corporation as the main social and economic organizing unit of our time. 2008 was the year the earth went urban: today, more than half the world's population lives in urban areas. And that's growing all the time. Our great cities and mega-regions are more important even than countries: the world's forty largest mega-regions account for two-thirds of the global economy and nine in ten of our technological innovations. Mayors and local leaders have become key figures navigating the global economy.

The rise of an increasingly urban world poses some of the greatest challenges of our time. Housing, safety, public transportation, utilities, sustainability, the preservation of open space, and development – all fall under the domain of urban planning.

There's so much work to be done

to make our cities better places to live, work and breathe. How to develop new and better urban housing? How to retrofit declining strip malls and suburban subdivisions? How to make huge global cities greener, more sustainable and energy efficient? Who will figure out how to discourage exurban sprawl in the U.S. in a way that satisfies all residents? What can be done to help Detroit or other shrinking cities like Flint and Youngstown? How can we change housing policy so that our workforce can benefit from greater mobility? How to make sure growing cities like San Francisco, Seattle and DC don't become completely gentrified—how to ensure affordable housing is available to maintain diversity? Even questions like how can we shape immigration policies so that we can continue to draw the best and brightest from a global talent pool? If one stays flexible and adaptable to the changing landscape, there's really

no limit to the impact one can have on these pressing problems.

Inspiring work is being done everywhere. Shrinking cities like Flint, Michigan, are experimenting with adopt-a-lot programs, in which vacant lots are taken over by neighborhood residents and kept clean and green. Booming cities like New York are creating pedestrian-friendly spaces that unclog traffic-choked streets. If you've seen the long car-free stretches of Broadway, or leisurely sat in the city-provided chairs that have taken over the very spaces where cars once idled in 24-7 traffic jams, you've experienced firsthand the power of an urban planner's vision. And in academia, even behavioral neuroscientists such as Collin Ellard—author of *You Are Here*—are exploring ways to make cities of all sizes both more efficient and more intuitive.

I say go for it. There is really no better time for this calling.

Introduction

by Tim Halbur, Managing Editor, Planetizen

When I was about 34, I was more than ten years into a career in media production. I'd done everything I'd wanted to do as a producer, and was ready for a change. I stumbled upon a book called *Home from Nowhere* by James Howard Kunstler, which led me to realize that the environment that had been built around me—from the cul-de-sac I grew up on to the quaint San Francisco neighborhood where I was living—was the result of decisions made by urban planners, developers and architects.

Tim Halbur

"I really think for planning, that this is the time. The climate challenge, for example, is essentially a planning problem. Creating livable cities has, I think, never been more important. There is really no better time to be involved in these issues."

— Anthony Flint, Lincoln Institute of Land Policy

The more I read, and the more people I met who were working in the field, the more I became convinced that planning was where I needed to be. I made the decision to switch careers, and went back to school to get my master's degree in urban and regional planning.

Most people who work in urban planning have a story similar to this. Rarely does anyone leave high school with a clear path towards working in land use. It is a field that people are drawn into, following their passions to the inevitable conclusion that many of the issues that impact our society—energy use, transportation, infrastructure, architecture—intersect with wide-ranging consequences. Working in land use gives you the opportunity to work at that intersection.

What You Didn't Learn in School

While we have a great admiration for the schools teaching urban planning, most people coming out of planning school still have little understanding of the variety of career options available to them. Most programs focus on a particular subset of job types, like city and regional planner or urban designer. But out in the real world, a plethora of exciting careers is available for people interested in working in land use. This guide will give you an insider's look at these career options, from A (Architect) to Z (Zoning Administrator).

Universities can also be monocultural in outlook, communicating a particular political viewpoint and way of doing things. In reality, the world of urban planning encompasses a wide variety of views and perspectives on how land use and business should be conducted. Because urban planning is often seen as 'social engineering,' and certain strategies in vogue today are touted

Introduction

as solutions to problems like global warming, it is easy to assume that planners come from the liberal side of the political spectrum. In fact, the people working in land use have a range of backgrounds and political beliefs. Libertarians, for one, are quite vocal and involved in urban planning.

Developers ≠ Snidely Whiplash

It is also tempting for people new to the field to stereotype developers as the bad guys, twirling their mustaches and bilking poor people with their evil schemes. In fact, development is a rich area of practice that can range from non-profit affordable housing to green building to big box retail. Developers are also an essential part of creating new, vibrant communities, because without investment, the grand visions of city planners don't get built.

Public vs. Private Sector

The one thing that most city and regional planners will agree on is that it can take a very, very long time to see their work have an impact. The graphic above gives some indication as to why. Fashion, on top, moves quickly. Governance, towards the middle, moves very slowly, and for good reason. If government made decisions as quickly as fashion, people would be hesitant to build things, spend money and put down roots because rules would be constantly changing.

City planning is part of that world, a world of planning processes that take years to create, solicit feedback, approve, and, finally, implement. It can often be frustrating to be an individual trying to make a difference in a bureaucratic system like a city government. On the other hand, local government is where the power resides for decision-making on what goes where. So working for a city means you are working at the center of power.

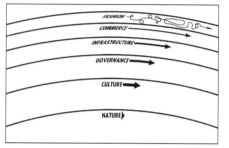

Private practice, on the other hand, works at the level of commerce and infrastructure, moving faster out of necessity. Where you fit in is all a matter of what type of personality you have and your tolerance for long-term vs. short-term rewards.

Geography is another significant difference between the public and private sectors. Planners, politicians, and commissioners benefit from a deep understanding of, and commitment to, a single place. El Cerrito, California City Councilor Ann Cheng (profiled on page 94), for example, gets a lot of satisfaction from focusing on her hometown and benefits in her job from having grown up there. In private practice on the other hand, you can get work all over the globe. Calthorpe and Associates, based in Berkeley, California, works in locations ranging from Austin, Texas, to Karnataka, India. Dubai and China have also been hotbeds of activity for American consultants.

As Paul Smoke writes in the following pages, while it is difficult to get work in planning departments in other countries due to differing laws, many private firms are finding work at the international level, particularly at larger firms. If working internationally is of interest to you, you might consider looking into a career with firms like Arup, HDR or HNTB. If you're invested deeply in making change at the local level, a career as a city planner may be the right choice.

Job Growth and Contraction

U.S. News and World Report named Urban and Regional Planner one of the "Best Careers for 2009." Planetizen regulars found this a bit ironic when city coffers were drying up and planning departments across the country were cutting jobs. Most cities lean heavily on property and/or sales taxes to fund their operations, and with the loss of property value, rampant foreclosures, and contracting consumer spending, cities were facing a steep cut in revenue. Ocala, Florida trimmed almost 100 jobs from its planning staff, and Petaluma, California eliminated its entire planning department.

As of this writing, the job market appears to be on the rise. Economic stimulus money from the Obama Administration is wending its way through the process to fund infrastructure improvements and is starting to reach cities, counties and states. With a significant focus on transportation improvements, it seems likely that transportation planners will be in high demand in the near future. Private planning firms will also likely see increasing demand in the coming years.

Dena Belzer of Strategic Economics, an urban economics research and consulting firm, agrees that the ups and downs of the economy can create a seesaw effect between public and private planning. "During economic downturns, cities are typically more worried about economic development and specifically about maintaining and/or growing their tax base," writes Belzer. "In all of the downturns I've been through, we saw our business remain stable or grow just because cities wanted to be more strategic about tying land use decisions to tax revenue generation, and trying to ensure that the local economy would still be robust as the economy worked its way through the current cycle." But, Belzer says, the development-driven side of her work has taken a significant hit because of the lack of any significant real estate activity. This slowdown is impacting all segments of the consulting industry related to land planning and development, including land planners, transportation planners/engineers, and urban economists. But conditions are even worse in the public sector, where so many more people have lost their jobs.

Stay Flexible

One of the great secrets of having a career is learning to ride out the ups and downs of the market. By staying flexible and not too fixed on one job (say, city planner), you might find that you are more fulfilled and better balanced. For example, you may be happy working part-time in a nonprofit advocating for better local transit and part-time as a subcontractor on NEPA requirements. There will always be times when one specialty is more in demand than others. The trick is knowing when to make the leap—like Anthony Flint (profiled on page 108), who left his job as an urban affairs journalist for a think tank just in time to avoid the collapse of the newspaper business.

See the Entire Spectrum

City planning doesn't happen in a void, and there is a significant amount of careers on the periphery that go overlooked by new students and graduates. We hope that this book will give you an understanding of the breadth of the field so you can focus your education and work experience towards the job that will be most fulfilling for you.

And the story doesn't end here—visit us at www.planetizen.com for up-to-date news and information on careers in urban planning, and visit our extended multimedia section of the book at planetizen.com/insiders.

Planning in Developing Countries

By Paul Smoke
Professor of Public Finance and Planning and Director of International Programs
New York University, Robert F. Wagner Graduate School of Public Service

As a broad based and applied field, graduates of master's programs in urban planning can find interesting and varied job opportunities in developing countries. At the same time, there are some differences between the job markets for urban planners in the developing world, both in terms of the context in which planners typically operate and the planning-related skills that are most highly valued. There are a few points that planners might wish to consider when investigating working in developing countries, with the caveat that these countries are highly diverse, ranging from more highly developed to very weak/fragile/post-conflict/in-conflict states that pose particularly great challenges.

First, some core skills taught to planners in western countries are often not those most valuable to developing countries. Land use planning, for example, is built on legal and land tenure systems that may differ greatly from what a planner would study in North America or Europe. These systems also vary across developing countries, most of which have relevant local capacity. This is not to say that traditional planning skills are unimportant or not useful, but demand for external expertise is more likely to target knowledge and skills that are not more readily available domestically. These could include, for example, institutional development and governance (including participatory planning in weak civil society environments), as well as technical skills, such as urban public finance/financial management, urban management and GIS.

Second, the roles of planners in developing countries may be spread in various ways across multiple levels of government. Although democratization and decentralization in recent years have been changing the situation, it was long typical in many countries for traditional urban planning tasks and functions, such as preparation of conventional master plans, to be primarily undertaken or heavily managed by a central government ministry of planning, local government, land use, urban development, public works, etc. Local government planning authorities are increasingly more independent in some countries, but in many cases, they remain partly or heavily managed and financed by central agencies, including multiple sectoral ministries with national mandates for specific public services. Thus, urban planning graduates who want to work in a developing country need to be prepared to work in complex, multi-level accountability environments that often differ in non-trivial ways from what they would typically face in industrialized countries.

Third, it is not very common for national and local agencies or planning firms in developing countries to directly hire western-trained urban planners. The opportunities for foreigners are greater through international development agencies—multilaterals, such as the World Bank, the regional development banks, or the United Nations; bilaterals, such as the US Agency for International Development (USAID); the private sector firms and think tanks that multilateral and bilateral international development agencies often contract to do work in particular countries; or nongovernmental organizations (NGOs) that work on issues related to subnational (regional, urban or rural) development and governance. The nature and relative levels of involvement of these external agencies may vary considerably across countries. Thus, planners who want to work in developing countries need to think whether they are more interested in working with particular types of organizations or in certain regions or countries, and they will need to explore the specific opportunities available that meet their priorities.

Finally, it is very useful for planners who wish to work in developing countries to have some background in political economy and social/cultural analysis. Political and social aspects of planning are universally important, and few contemporary planners see themselves purely as technicians. At the same time, the nature of social/cultural realities and political/bureaucratic dynamics in developing countries—with often low levels of institutional development, weak accountability and limited capacity—may pose special or more binding challenges. Planners working in such contexts need to understand these realities and dynamics in order to work effectively.

Planners can look to various sources of information and advice on international development planning careers. These include professional associations, international agencies and financial institutions, job services, think tanks and consulting firms. The American Planning Association offers an international page on its website (www. planning.org/international/index.htm) and has an International Division (www.planning.org/divisions/international/index.htm). The Association of Collegiate Schools of Planning (www.acsp.org) has a Global Planners Education Interest Group (www.gpeig. org) which provides links to non-US planning associations. Another useful resource on international planning associations is the Global Planners Network (www.globalplannersnetwork.org).

Many international agencies engage in urban initiatives. The World Bank operates an Urban Division (www.worldbank.org) and supports the Cities Alliance (www. citiesalliance.org/ca); key UN agencies include the Center for Human Settlements (UNCHS-Habitat, www.unchs.org), UN Development Program (www.undp.org) and UN Capital Development Fund (www. uncdf.org). Some bilateral agencies support programs of interest to planners, including USAID (www.usaid.gov/our_work/economic_growth_and_trade/urban_programs) and they sometimes develop separate websites on specific relevant initiatives, such as USAID's Making Cities Work (www.makingcitieswork.org).

A number of job search sites focus on international (www.jobsabroad.com) or international development (www.devex. com/jobs), and they on occasion run dedicated articles on planning (http://devex. com/articles/urban-planning-jobs-what-you-need-to-know). Finally, major consulting firms on international development include AECOM (www.aecom.com); Abt Associates (www.abtassociates.com), Development Alternatives International (www.dai.com); Research Triangle Institute (www.rti.org/page.cfm/International_Development), and Associates in Rural Development (www. ardinc.com). Many other large consulting firms do international work and may have field offices in developing regions.

Working as a planner in developing countries can be enormously productive, interesting and rewarding. Prospective international development planners should go into this exciting line of work aware of the realities and opportunities involved, and they need to be committed to operating in a way that can help to bring about genuine and sustainable results in often complex and unfamiliar environments.

Careers

Planning

The City of Raleigh, North Carolina's Planning Department at work.

Whether you want to call it city planning, urban planning, urban design, or any number of names, the act of planning is both simple to understand and enormously complex to execute. Within the field there is a lot of understanding and discussion about what it means to plan, but for many unfamiliar with the insider's jargon, what we mean by "planning" is not exactly clear.

Planning is a broad field, encompassing a variety of duties and purposes. To many, it simply means city-building. In this light, a layperson may believe that most of our present-day cities don't have any more planning to do. They are already built, and people live there – what more planning could they need? This perception makes sense if we think of planning as the early, historical city layout sessions that decided where streets should lie and where people should settle. This is a role of planning, but does not fully encompass the field.

Contrary to this layperson's perception, there is a lot of planning going on today, and a lot of planners planning. Every city and community is in a constant state of flux and evolution. There is no final resting point for a city, and recent population growth and changes in the global climate highlight how the places we live must be flexible and reactionary. Planners—those who plan—recognize this. These are people who care about how cities work. They try to understand how cities can be created, maintained and improved. Planners are everywhere, and they are needed everywhere.

City Planner

The U.S. Department of Labor defines planning as the practice of developing strategies for using land and managing the growth and revitalization of the world's cities and communities. From the description: "Planners promote the best use of a community's land and resources for residential, commercial, institutional, and recreational purposes. They address environmental, economic, and social health issues of a community as it grows and changes."

The professional membership organization for planners, the American Planning Association, defines planning as "a dynamic profession that works to improve the welfare of people and their communities by creating more convenient, equitable, healthful, efficient, and attractive places for present and future generations. Planning enables civic leaders, businesses, and citizens to play a meaningful role in creating communities that enrich people's lives."

These definitions are apt. They capture much of what the practice is and why it exists. But they don't quite get to the essence of what it means to plan. In essence, planning is a juggling act.

City planners have a variety of responsibilities as they attempt to serve the public in all its diverse forms. They work with the physical form of cities by defining and controlling the use of land, the way it is developed, how it grows, where it begins and where it ends. This physical manifestation of planning is one of the most contentious aspects of the field—how land is divided up and used and reused tends to create a fiery debate amongst such groups as homeowners, politicians, advocacy groups, city officials, developers, environmentalists and so on. At any time, nearly any possible combination of these groups may be working with or against each other to make sure some development is not approved or some land acquisition is allowed. Planners deal with these competing forces on a daily basis, and oftentimes what is best for the community is not what any of the stakeholding groups had in mind.

Another role planners play is to deal with people—not just in the sense of trying to make people happy politically, but trying to create communities that people enjoy living in, visiting, and experiencing. Much of this human-focused work tends to revolve around housing. Planners define what type of housing goes where and how much of it there will be. They've also got to worry about locating goods and services for the people their cities are made of, and ensure that the people can travel in between their various Point As and Point Bs. Creating cities and places with good mobility is one of the biggest challenges facing planners in the 21st century. Making sure that cities can sustain their populations, their levels of quality and their economies is the heart of planning.

The day-to-day world of a city planner will likely involve many tasks and projects, from reviewing development proposals to approving zoning variances to preparing reports for public meetings. City planners tend to wear many hats and carry a diverse set of skills. They not only have a deep understanding of how their municipality's development process works, but also how it fits in with the rest of the local government operation and the ultimate goals of the community. By working on both the minor details and the bigger picture, city planners help citizens and officials to enact the policies and build the projects that make communities better.

Amanda Burden, FAICP

Director, New York City Department of City Planning
Chair, New York City Planning Commission

Planetizen: Tell us about your career path. How did you get to where you are now?

AB: In the early 1980s, I became the Vice President for Planning and Design for the Battery Park City Authority in Lower Manhattan, where I was in charge of developing and implementing a master plan for the site as well as designing the waterfront esplanade and 30 acres of public open space.

When I started, there were 92 acres of sand to be transformed into a place people would want to be. The master plan integrated the site into the fabric of Lower Manhattan, thus alleviating the perception of discontinuity that had made developers reluctant to build. The design focus was on creating great public spaces that were vibrant, livable and inviting. That legacy has made Battery Park City one of the most economically successful large scale urban development projects in the country.

I was appointed to the City Planning Commission in 1990, where I served as a member for 12 years before Mayor Michael Bloomberg appointed me as the director of the agency and chair of the commission. Since my appointment, we have undertaken a huge work plan—rezoning nearly a fifth of the city, creating capacity for a million more people, putting underutilized land and buildings to work as part of the mayor's Five Borough Economic Opportunity Plan, reclaiming our waterfront for public use, while preserving the neighborhoods that are the heart and soul of the city. We are shaping a blueprint for the future of the city, carefully, intelligently block by block, street by street, while ensuring that New York City continues to grow as a world city of opportunity.

Planetizen: Describe a typical day in your current position.

AB: My days start early and just aren't long enough. For all of our large-scale plans, it is essential to understand the constraints and opportunities in each neighborhood and to build from the characteristic strengths of each one. Therefore, I spend an enormous amount of time walking neighborhood streets, working directly with communities to understand firsthand their concerns, helping them understand our proposals and building consensus toward an implementable vision that builds on their strengths. You have to invest the time to develop their trust and to design a plan that meets their needs.

Planetizen: What do you like best about your position?

AB: I feel very fortunate to be able to work on designing the greatest city in the world with a mayor who understands that good design is good economic development and is essential to the long term health and sustainability of the city. One of my favorite and one of the most successful projects I have worked on is the High Line, an abandoned elevated rail line that has now been transformed into one of the most unique parks in the world. It is not only visually magical—a wild garden in the sky—it has also become the defining feature of a new neighborhood. Through a combination of extraordinary advocacy, zoning innovation and mayoral vision and commitment, the High Line/West Chelsea plan has succeeded in transforming the High Line, in preserving the city's premier art gallery district and in creating an economically integrated neighborhood. Seeing the park finally open to the public was my proudest moment as commissioner.

Planetizen: What is most challenging about your job?

AB: Our challenge has been finding places for the city to grow, while at the same time preserving and building on the unique character of individual neighborhoods. Essentially, we want the city to grow, but not change. We have done so by channeling growth to transit-rich areas by using urban design master plans as an integral component of zoning, and by ensuring that every development has a dynamic connection to the street.

Planetizen: How has your perception of the field changed since you first entered the planning and development community?

AB: What's really different is that when I was in planning school, the future of places like New York was very much in doubt. The country was suburbanizing and dense cities were seen as modern-day dinosaurs. Today,

successful cities like New York, San Francisco or Boston are thriving so we have to respond to the challenges of growth instead of the challenges of decline.

Planetizen: What do you wish you'd known about planning when you were starting out?

AB: There is no such thing as successful planning without real, ongoing community involvement. An engaged community makes a neighborhood work. No one has all the answers—not planners, not governments, not even community groups or citizens. Good plans, real plans that can do their job of making people's lives better, come from the often tedious, often frustrating, always complex and iterative process of involving everyone who has a stake in the community.

Planetizen: What advice would you give to someone interested in becoming a city planner?

AB: Listen. Understanding the community you are working with is essential to being a good planner. Being a planner requires a vision of what a place should be for its people as well as passion, persuasion and execution. Walk the streets. You can't a make a plan for a place without knowing that place intimately and viscerally. A vibrant streetlife is the spirit of a neighborhood—you can't get a sense of it from pictures or through the windows of a car. Your responsibility is to help people make their communities stronger, healthier and more alive. You are abdicating your professional and moral responsibilities if you try to make changes to a neighborhood that you have not taken the time to get to know. Finally, one must know how to translate that vision into reality.

Kyle Kritz

Associate Planner, City of Dubuque, Iowa

Planetizen: How did you choose to go into planning?

KK: At the time I started my undergrad degree, most of the graduates of geography or geology got jobs in the oil industry, in education or sometimes with the National Park Service. By the time I graduated, it was kind of another recession like we're going through now. The price of oil was at $16.00 a barrel, so nobody was hiring in the oil industry. I was really on a track to do teaching, but there wasn't much available for geography.

I talked to an Air Force recruiter, and they were very interested in me coming to the Air Force and working with the satellite imagery program that they were getting started at that time, back in the early '80s. I signed the papers and I got actually one day in the Air Force and they did a third physical and they found out that the knee I had injured back when I was 17 years old really was a problem, so I was in the Air Force for one day before they washed me out.

Then I was back at the University of Iowa on campus and actually looked in the course catalog. The university didn't have an undergraduate degree in planning, only a master's degree in planning, so I applied for that and got in. I mostly studied transportation and economic development. But the whole time I was in the master's program, I worked for the city of Iowa City as an intern in the planning office, where I got large cross-section of working with the other planners, involving community development, transportation

and then also zoning. After graduating with my master's degree, my first job was with the village of Skokie, Illinois, which is right on the north border of the city of Chicago. I was there for a couple of years, but Skokie being an inner suburb, there wasn't a whole lot of land left to develop. It was a very interesting place, but there wasn't as much work to do as I would have liked. So I wound up working for the city of Dubuque next, which is where I've been for the last 18 years.

Dubuque had one of the highest unemployment rates in the country in the early '80s. Now, Dubuque has been very fortunate and very successful since the mid-'80s in positioning itself to expand the number of jobs and diversify the local economy from being just centered on manufacturing and meat packaging. Now we're actually attracting a lot more tech jobs.

Planetizen: What is a typical day for you?

KK: It's very deadline-oriented. We have monthly meetings with our zoning commission and zoning board of adjustments. Two meetings a month with city council, weekly meetings on development and review committees. Everything that we do almost on a daily basis is focused on those deadlines, including getting notifications out to neighbors and to the paper. Any day you walk in, it's basically how many days left to get this done, this out, that kind of thing. To some extent it's somewhat regimented. The cases change, but after 18 years there's a lot of similarity.

Then, obviously, there's the emails and the calls that come in, whether they be questions for code enforcement, questions on flood plains, questions on zoning, questions on development that the assistant planners and I spend a good portion of our day either responding to by phone or email.

Planetizen: What do you like best about your work? What do you find the most challenging?

KK: Actually a lot of times it's the same for both. It's working with the public on the growth and development and redevelopment of the community. It's very interesting working with citizens, with the commissioners and the elected officials.

It can be challenging too, trying to provide the information and the guidance that they're expecting from us in a way that works for them. Understanding that people have different abilities and come with different backgrounds, trying to not only serve their needs but also the greater communities as well.

Some Significant Employers *(in alphabetical order)*

City of Chicago Department of Planning and Development
https://chicago.taleo.net/careersection/100/jobsearch.ftl?lang=en

City of Houston Planning and Development Department, http://agency.governmentjobs.com/houston

City of Los Angeles Community Development Department, www.lacity.org/CDD/man_hr.html

City of Miami Planning Department, www.miamigov.com/planning

City of Phoenix Planning Department, http://phoenix.gov/jobs

City of Portland Bureau of Planning and Sustainability, www.portlandonline.com/bps

New York City Department of City Planning, www.ci.nyc.ny.us/html/dcp/html/about/joblist.shtml

Sample Job Description

Job Title: Senior Neighborhood Planner
Job Type: Planning
Date Posted: 12/01/2008
Organization: City of Denton, TX
URL: www.cityofdenton.com

Definition: Requires advanced professional planning experience of high complexity and variety; some functions are similar to those of the regular Senior Planner, though the Neighborhood Planner often leads or is significantly involved with neighborhood or community planning projects. The Neighborhood planner may supervise Planning technicians, Assistant Planners, and/or Associate Planners.

Essential Job Functions:

- Performs advanced planning and organizing techniques to assist with a wide variety of neighborhood activities, promoting citizen involvement in neighborhood issues, and serves as a liaison between various city departments such as Planning, Code Enforcement, Building Inspections and Community Development and citizens; advanced knowledge of the philosophies, principals, practices and techniques of neighborhood planning
- Understands and applies professional planning theories and principles, including but not limited to, statistical methods, land use planning, neighborhood planning, transportation planning, urban design, and public participation
- Guides and supports neighborhood stakeholders toward capacity building and training programs, and can lead and facilitate neighborhood meetings and action planning sessions to problem solve and build consensus
- Performs advanced professional work related to the development and implementation of small area plans

Minimum Qualifications:

- Master's degree in Urban Planning or related field and four years of professional planning experience.

OR

- Bachelor's degree in planning or related field and six years professional planning experience with at least two years experience in planning, developing, and leading neighborhood capacity building efforts.

OR

- Any combination of related education, experience, certifications and licenses that will result in successfully performing the essential functions of the job.

Salary: $4,041-$4,958/mo DOQ

More Resources

- American Planning Association, www.planning.org
- Project for Public Spaces, www.pps.org
- Congress for the New Urbanism, www.cnu.org
- Urban Land Institute, www.uli.org
- *The High Cost of Free Parking,* by Donald Shoup

Regional Planner

A Regional Planner develops short- and long-term plans regarding land use that relate to the issues of metropolitan regions as a whole. Public sector regional planners are employed by either MPOs (Metropolitan Planning Organizations) or COGs (Councils of Governments).

As cities expanded throughout the 20th century, their borders bumped into small towns, suburbs and other local governments, and in some cases, swallowed them whole. Conflicts arose between neighboring cities and towns, particularly over transit and highway routes, but also over placement of big box retail, sewage treatment, affordable housing, etc. Regional planning entities were created to resolve these differences and broker decisions for the region as a whole.

The daily activities of a regional planner can be divided into two main categories: policy analysis and liasing with governmental entities. Policy analysis can include developing a regional transportation plan (RTP) or regional housing needs allocations (RHNA), reports that can carry a lot of weight in how funds are distributed throughout the region. In preparing these documents, regional planners use geographic information systems (GIS), analyze trends and surveys, and collate data on commuting behaviors, health and obesity, and housing needs.

If you are interested in advising and working with mayors, city managers, and other high-level city officials, a job in regional planning could be for you. In few other careers in planning do you get access to decisionmakers so often and quickly. The regional planner works directly with officials who sit on committees and councils to make decisions like how to implement car pool lanes, where affordable housing will get built, how to reduce auto emissions and where to build light rail stations.

Of course, direct access to power does not mean that a regional planner gains power themselves. As Ted Droettboom notes in his profile on page 10, land use decisions still reside with local juridictions. Mayors can come to council meetings, get reports ad nauseam from planners about the regional good, and then decide (quite rationally) to go with the immediate needs of their local constituents over the good of the whole region.

Portland, Oregon's regional agency, Metro, is unusual in that it is the only directly-elected metropolitan planning organization in the United States. It was established in 1978 by a statewide ballot measure. Metro, therefore, has more direct power to implement policy and can even dictate land use policy to local towns and cities. Metro's most prominent roles are managing the urban growth boundary and the regional transportation system.

As you may have guessed by now, transportation is often a big part of a regional planner's job. That's because the connective tissue of the region is the street, and people need the ability to get around between cities and towns. When creating bus lines or light rail, each area the line passes through will want to be involved in decisions like where the bus stops get built and whether the rail goes underground or not. Regional transportation planners are often negotiating with local governments on these sorts of issues so that transit and freeways can be most effective. Regional planners also work directly with the people in those communities to get their input on regional plans and educate them about the decisions being made.

Ted Droettboom

Regional Planning Program Director

Planetizen: Can you describe your job for us?

TD: I am the relationship counselor for four agencies that are learning to live together, which is to say I try to get the staffs of those agencies to agree on common work, to take on that work in an integrated, mutually supportive manner, where there are issues of policy that affects one or more of the agencies to serve as a policy maker forum where those issues can be resolved, sort of like a conference committee between two houses of a legislature.

Planetizen: What do you see as the challenges of working as a regional planner?

TD: The principal challenges are that in all regions in this country, with one exception, land use authority and control, which is a big part of planning, rests solely as a responsibility of local governments themselves. There is no direct authority over zoning or plans or anything that actually affects where in the end development occurs. So the regional land use planning function is entirely voluntary and advisory, and frequently the regional interest, the collective interest, is not necessarily the same as the aggregated interest of the individual localities. Consequently there is always a tension between those interests.

Planetizen: Our understanding is that regional government influences decisions by using carrots and sticks (incentives and penalties).

TD: It's mostly carrots. Although Larry Dahms (former executive director of the Metropolitan Transportation Commission)

used to say, "A carrot is only a stick painted orange." If you give carrots to some, it means you're denying it from others, in which case they become sticks. But in truth the most significant regional planning authority that exists in this region is the allocation of transportation funds, and those could be regarded mostly as carrots. There are no significant restrictions on development, for example, or ways of encouraging development other than providing carrots.

Planetizen: By definition, it seems that regional planners get to think "bigger picture" than local planners, who can get mired at the project and building level. In your experience, is that true?

TD: Yes and no. Particularly in California where there is not a lot of general revenue to fund planning at either the citywide or neighborhood level, and a lot of planning departments are essentially run as enterprises funded from development permit revenue, local planners will primarily deal with individual projects. Still, a significant number of them, particularly in the better funded municipalities, will in fact do citywide or neighborhood-wide planning and really look beyond the next project and look at how the city works and how the city can improve.

The principal interest in doing the regional stuff is in fact, increasingly the "real city", and the real "city state", is at the metropolitan regional level. We live metropolitanly. We frequently live in one place and work in another. We recreate all around the region. We share a common media market, and, increasingly, a sense of a bigger place than just the city or town or county in which we live. And there are clear, very important issues, most of them related to the regional transportation system, that require a regional look. The biggest example of that is greenhouse gases resulting from transportation emissions. You cannot deal with those by just doing it city by city, because transportation requires an origin and a destination. And that's a big, important problem, as is the relationship with urban areas and their rural hinterlands. The farmland and other open space resources that people

enjoy as a region require regional management. So there's a whole bunch of significant issues which just simply are not manageable purely at the local government level and are not efficiently managed at the state level. You need to bring together local interests, regional interests and state interests, and the regional agencies are the appropriate meeting places for that to happen.

Planetizen: What path would you recommend for people interested in a career in regional planning?

TD: I would actually recommend that folks interested in regional planning don't go directly into regional planning, because most of what you're going to be doing is interacting with local governments. I think it helps to understand their perspective by working for local governments for at least a few years to know the kinds of issues they face so you can put them in a regional context, and understand what those folks have to deal with, and understand why sometimes they are less interested in your abstract notions of regional planning as you think they should be.

Some Significant Employers *(in alphabetical order)*

Association of Bay Area Governments (ABAG)/Metropolitan Transportation Commission (MTC) www.abag.ca.gov/jobs.html, www.mtc.ca.gov/jobs

Chicago Metropolitan Agency for Planning (CMAP), www.cmap.illinois.gov/careers.aspx

Oregon Metro, www.oregonmetro.gov

Regional Plan Association (NY/NJ/CT), www.rpa.org

Sample Job Description

Job Title: Regional Planner
Job Type: Planning
Date Posted: 03/31/2009
Organization: The Miami Valley Regional Planning Commission
URL: www.mvrpc.org

The Miami Valley Regional Planning Commission is accepting applications for a Regional Transportation Planner.

MVRPC serves an innovative multi-county region of approximately one million people in the area surrounding Dayton, Ohio (southwest Ohio). The agency provides planning services to member jurisdictions, and also functions as the MPO for the Dayton area.

The position is part of a planning team responsible for preparing the regional long range transportation plan and assisting in special studies. Duties include participation in development of the long range plan, including public involvement activities and coordination with member jurisdictions and regulatory agencies. Additional duties include collecting, maintaining, analyzing transportation and land use data under a GIS environment, technical data analysis, report writing and the ability to effectively summarize the data for presentations.

The position requires considerable knowledge of transportation and land use planning; skill in the use of GIS software (ArcMap); some experience with transportation planning/capacity software a plus. Must possess demonstrated experience with: strong research and technical writing skills; ability to gather, organize, and analyze information/data of a technical nature; effective oral/written/presentation communication skills; ability to deal effectively with the public; proficient in Word, Access, and Excel; and must possess a valid current driver's license (field work required). Transportation planning experience is preferred.

Qualifications: Bachelor's degree in planning, urban studies, geography, or related field, master's degree preferred, with minimum of two years of related experience, preferably with a public entity.

Starting salary to be determined DOQ. Submit a cover letter and resume via e-mail to personnel@mvrpc.org or via regular mail to Personnel, Miami Valley Regional Planning Commission, One Dayton Centre, One South Main Street, Suite 260, Dayton, OH 45402.

More Resources

- National Association of Regional Councils, www.narc.org
- Metropolitan Growth Planning in California, 1900-2000, a report from the Public Policy Institute of California, www.ppic.org/main/publication.asp?i=191
- Bureau of Labor Statistics, 2008-09, www.bls.gov/oco/ocos057.htm

Federal Planner

Planning, by its nature, is a very local process. It deals with neighborhoods, streets, and specific communities. So when one thinks of the job title "federal planner," the sheer scale it suggests is almost contrary to the local-ness of planning.

We're not often aware of it, but large swaths of land in the U.S. are controlled by the federal government. Federal planners are simply planning what gets built (or not) on that land, from national parks to government facilities to military installations. Like city planners, federal planners handle comprehensive planning and land management policies for properties, only on a larger scale and usually with fewer people living on the land.

The Department of Transportation has the largest number of federal community planners. They try to address the problems that exist and anticipate what will be needed in the future to handle changes in demand. States and metropolitan planning organizations typically handle the specific allocations of money, but because most of the funding for transportation projects comes from the federal government, it is the policies at the top that determine where and for what this money goes. Federal transportation planners craft these policies.

Aside from transportation, much of the work in the federal planning sector is related to the military. Often the size of small cities, military bases are pretty much just like any other municipality in terms of planning. Populations grow, housing needs change, and mobility patterns evolve,

creating the need for planners to craft the land use policies and decisions that react appropriately.

Just as cities are leaning more towards mixed-use development and sustainable communities, military bases are increasingly updating their land use decisions to create more livable places. The idea of the walkable town center, for example, is gathering popularity amongst military base planners, highlighting the parallel planning paths of military installations and cities.

But because military installations and other federal lands are not cities, there is a physical clash when they meet. The borders around these sites are typically a focus for federal planners. Balancing the needs of the military with the needs of the surrounding community can be a challenge. For example, a large Air Force testing ground is going to have a lot of air traffic and loud sounds. Reducing the impact on neighboring communities and smoothing ruffled feathers is an important part of the job, particularly when the site is on foreign soil among a culture with different expectations.

Day to day, a federal planner will engage in typical planning activities, from updating master plans to communicating with clients. The job will be similar to that of traditional municipal planners, but often through the lens of the military establishment. But despite the audience, the purpose of a federal planner's job is the same as any others: to guide growth and development, to address the needs of residents ,and to ensure the long-term sustainability of the community.

Mark Sanchez

Community Planner, Air Force Center for Engineering and Environment

Planetizen: Describe what an Air Force community planner does.

MS: Base community planners have two large work elements that relate to and reinforce each other. The first is what I call base comprehensive planning. And that is the comprehensive planning process that is reflected in the document that they put out for the base, called the base general plan. This should all ring familiar to city and town planners, who do the very same sort of thing, as they put out their jurisdiction's general plan or comp plan or master plan.

The second one is what we affectionately refer to as the "encroachment work program." The main goals is to be kinder to our neighbors and reduce any negative impacts of the base on the surrounding area. Essentially, it's regional planning – working with their local government colleagues to sustain the base within the regional setting.

Planetizen: Describe a typical day at your job.

MS: Well, that's the fun part; I don't think it's greatly dissimilar from life in local government planning departments. Of course, I can say that having spent some time in local government, state government before coming on with the Feds.

A key difference is we're typically not staffed at an Air Force base like a large city planning department. We may be more like the small town, or the village, in the sense that you may see a base community planner or perhaps two of them at an installation. They have to field the entire work program of issues and where they can make the best

use of consultant resources to help them as well. I'd say it's like the small town doctor, jack-of-all-trades, master of none, and if the specialist is needed then you reach out for the support at that time.

I've heard Air Force leaders, senior officers, describe this practice as probably one of the, if not *the* most interesting job on an air force installation. Other than, say, perhaps the base commander himself. It's been very gratifying over the years when base commanders lift up and highlight their base community planners as the ultimate stewards for wise sustainable development of the military installation.

Planetizen: What is the most challenging part of your job?

MS: I guess I come back to the staffing question again, coming from my experience in local government, state government, certainly in the state agency. I came from a division where we had 50, 60 planners on the staff. There, projects were approached with matrix teams, cross-functional teams. It seemed in the state agency we didn't go to a meeting without two people there. Then to come to the Air Force, where many of our bases have only one or two planners there, was a big difference.

Therefore, in my opinion, it can create a situation with high, high burnout potential. As a few years pass, for younger planners, the grind of controversial issues, incessant phone calls and emails, evening meetings with city councils and planning and zoning commissions and so forth – which air force planners do too, especially in that regional planning work element – all of that can really get to you. We spend a lot of time off the military installations informing city councils, and planning and zoning commissions about the impacts of incompatible development.

That burnout potential highlights the need for federal planners be talented at figuring out quickly what's important now – keeping their eyes on the horizon, to borrow an Air Force expression.

Planetizen: what advice would you offer them to someone who is interested in becoming a federal planner?

MS: When I talk to young planners expressing interest in coming to work for the military, I usually begin by having a conversation about socialization in the military. Because the military has a culture. And this is not to suggest anything good, bad or indifferent, it is just a different culture. I try to get a sense if that individual might or might not be a good fit for the military and its particular hierarchical, bureaucracy, decision making apparatus. So I have to ask: "Would you be comfortable working within the military architecture?"

Some may challenge me and say, "Well, dealing with a small-town mayor, is it that different?" You know, the mayor is usually just a part-time elected official or temporary elected official. Councilmen are the same, and they may be elected and put in office by certain sectors in the community. And if the young planner would recognize that, then yes indeed, then you should adapt well to working within the military structure.

Many times, a person, similar to myself, will have had prior military experience, served in the service, retired, served in the Guard, National Reserve, spouse in the service. And that's a great start because then they've been somewhat socialized in the system.

Some Significant Employers *(in alphabetical order)*

Federal Emergency Management Agency, www.fema.gov

U.S. Army Corps of Engineers, www.usace.army.mil

U.S. Department of Transportation, Federal Transit Administration
www.fta.dot.gov/planning_environment.html

Sample Job Description

Job Title: Military Planner
Job Type: Planning
Date Posted: 07/20/2009
Organization: Mead & Hunt, Inc.
URL: www.meadhunt.com

Mead & Hunt, a highly successful and recognized national consulting firm, is experiencing unprecedented growth. Because of our success, we are seeking a highly motivated experienced military planner. Responsibilities will include functioning as lead planner on complex military master plans, area development plans, and special studies; project management, and client management. This position is located in our Vancouver, Washington (Portland area) office and will require travel.

The successful candidate must possess a bachelor's degree (or higher) in planning, architecture, landscape architecture, engineering, or a field related to planning and at least five years of relevant planning experience.

The ideal candidate will have any/all of the following: master's degree with emphasis in physical or developmental planning from an accredited college or university; military, campus, and/or neighborhood planning experience; working knowledge of DOD/Air Force/Army planning, facilities management, real property records, military regulations; familiarity and/or experience with FAA airport master planning and/or airport layout plans; familiarity and/or experience with alternative energy systems, environmental compliance; AICP certification; LEED certification; GIS experience; aptitude and willingness to work with and make presentations to the public; articulate oral and written communication skills.

Mead & Hunt offers competitive salaries and benefits, a pleasant work environment, and excellent career opportunities. If you are interested in this exciting and challenging position, submit your cover letter and resume to the address below. Interviews will be awarded on our review of your ability to meet the qualifications listed in the above paragraphs describing the "successful" candidate and "ideal" candidate, so explain in your letter how you meet each qualification.

More Resources

- American Planning Association, Federal Planning Division, www.federalplanning.org
- National Association of State Facilities Administrators, www.nasfa.net
- USAF Center for Environmental Excellence, www.afcee.brooks.af.mil
- Office of the Deputy Under Secretary of Defense, Installations and Environment, www.acq.osd.mil/ie/index.shtml

Zoning Administrator

Zoning is where the rubber meets the road in city planning. City and regional planners create and evaluate land use development plans, but zoning constitutes the actual rules and code that makes those plans implementable.

The job of a zoning administrator (or zoning manager) is to make sure the city's zoning is in sync with the general plan, and that it is being implemented properly. In that respect, zoning administrators may also oversee code enforcement as well, which can mean monitoring building construction, blight, and nuisance.

In smaller towns and cities, zoning may not be a separate department from planning. Kirsten Sackett, for example, has a combined job with the City of Cortez, Colorado as a city planner/zoning administrator. "I make sure that all the requirements are followed and enforced in regards to the land use code," says Sackett, "and that people are informed when they have a violation. I'm looking at people having the wrong type of use, the sign code, things like that. But I'm also evaluating construction projects, updating the general plan, and doing city planner tasks."

The position is also quasi-judicial, in that the zoning administrator is often asked to interpret zoning requirements, area plan interpretations, and legal descriptions. "You have to be willing to listen to different opinions," says zoning administrator Roger Eastman (profiled next page). "Then formulate your own decision and then stick to it. I've had to deal with a number of appeals where I've made a decision that's been backed up by the city attorney, but not supported by the staff, or not supported by citizens or an applicant. That gets tough."

Over the past decade, it has become increasingly fashionable to discard traditional zoning in favor of "form-based codes." This new method of land use control rejects the zoning concept of separating certain uses (work, homes, retail) and instead focuses on the physical form of the buildings. In Petaluma, California, one of the first cities to adopt a form-based code, this has meant a transitionary tangle where the two codes competed for prominence. But with Miami, Florida recently becoming the first major city with a form-based code, this might be the wave of the future.

Whichever method you're dealing with, Leslie S. Pollock, AICP believes that zoning is essential to making great places. "A sense of place is more than the form of the place," wrote Pollock in an op-ed for Planetizen. "It is the function and level of activity that occurs there. Whether intended or not, the act of zoning can help to create or destroy the physical aspects of one's sense of place, because it is through zoning that a city regulates the way these placemaking elements come together."

There are also a number of positions in zoning in the private sector, particularly in the wireless telecommunications industry. A thorough understanding of zoning practice is valuable to such businesses.

Roger Eastman

Zoning Code Administrator, City of Flagstaff, Arizona

Planetizen: What does your job as a zoning administrator entail?

RE: My job is to create amendments to the code because the code is so dysfunctional. The major project right now is a half million dollar contract with a consulting firm to essentially rewrite our code to get rid of its complexity, its disjointed character, its lack of cohesiveness and make it a user-friendly, simple-to-understand code that applies uniquely to Flagstaff.

What we have is a general plan that is not consistent with the zoning ordinance. The general plan calls for essentially traditional neighborhood development: compact, mixed-use, walkable neighborhoods in Flagstaff. The zoning code is designed, as it exists right now, to create sprawl, auto-dominant type development. Hence the major disconnect, and why I have a wonderful job right now.

Planetizen: What was your career path?

RE: When I left school, I worked as a private consultant, but I didn't like it. I actually took off and guided photographic safaris for a while, got back to being a planning consultant and did some really fun work. I came to the United States and took a job with the city of Sedona, Arizona and I was eventually their senior planner managing all the new development through the process.

That was a dead-end job. Flagstaff offered this position under this title to do major code amendments, including writing a TND (traditional neighborhood development)

ordinance as a form-based code, and then the major rewrite of the city's zoning ordinance and that's what got me to where I am now because I work in a very engaging, proactive community who are not scared of taking on major challenges. That's really exciting to me, so I'm having a blast.

Planetizen: What do you see as the challenges of your position and what are the rewards?

RE: The challenges right now in terms of the major code rewrite is trying to find a way within the encumberances of Arizona law to rewrite the code to have it create smart growth and sustainable development in Flagstaff. That's a huge, huge challenge for us, but we've got a strong consulting team working with us.

So, as a project manager the challenge is blending the staff and consultants, and then dealing with a very schizophrenic citizenry, and ensuring that all aspects of the thought processes of our citizens are incorporated into a code so that nobody feels left out. That's a challenge. But, it is also extremely rewarding to be out talking to people, and getting their perspectives and trying to get people to come together. And, truly, we're making a difference in Flagstaff, and I'm leading that charge.

Planetizen: If you were giving advice to someone who was interested in a career as a zoning administrator what would you say? What kind of experience would you say they should get?

RE: I think you have to have a well-rounded experience. You've got to understand the long range planning side of it and the current planning side of it. And you have to be methodical in your approach to writing code, be a good code writer. Not everybody fits that category. And I'm proud to call myself a code geek. I love dealing with the details of writing or amending code because it's not that easy. You could say, "OK, we're going to rewrite our lighting ordinance. This is chapter, call it eight, of the code, but what's the impact in chapter five and chapter four and chapter sixteen?" What so often happens is in the rush to get an amendment through nobody thinks about the implications elsewhere. So, that's where the detail orientation comes from. You've really got to be interested and willing to spend the time to think things through. It's really problem solving at the basic level.

You have to be detail-oriented. You have to be logical. You have to be willing to listen to different opinions, and then formulate your own decision and then stick to it.

Some Significant Employers *(in alphabetical order)*

Boston Redevelopment Authority, www.bostonredevelopmentauthority.org/zoning/zoning.asp

City of Chicago's Zoning Department, http://maps.cityofchicago.org/website/zoning

Department of Consumer & Regulatory Affairs, District of Columbia, http://dcra.dc.gov

Little Rock, AK Planning Department, www.littlerock.org/CityDepartments/PlanningAndDevelopment

Miami Planning Department, www.miamigov.com/Planning/pages/community_planning

Minneapolis Planning Department, www.ci.minneapolis.mn.us/zoning

San Francisco Planning Department, www.sfgov.org/site/planning_index.asp

Wichita Planning Department, www.wichita.gov/CityOffices/Planning/Zoning

Sample Job Description

Job Title: Zoning Administrator
Job Type: Planning
Date Posted: 03/31/2009
Organization: City of Marshfield, Wisconsin
URL: http://ci.marshfield.wi.us

The purpose of the Planner/Zoning Administrator position is to administer the city zoning ordinances, as well as to assist the Director with planning and economic development related issues. Ordinance administration includes ordinance interpretation, review of requests for zoning changes, variances, conditional use permits, sign permits, and ordinance enforcement activities. Position duties also include overseeing the activities of the Zoning Board of Appeals. Planning-related duties include assisting the Director with short and long-range planning and economic development projects related to the Comprehensive Plan, boundary agreements, business and industrial park development and various special projects.

Essential Functions:

- Administers and enforces the City zoning ordinance. Responsible for reviewing requests for zoning changes, conditional use permits, variances, and sign permits to ensure conformity with the ordinance.
- Assists Director with planning-related projects such as the Comprehensive Plan, boundary agreements and assisting other departments with planning related projects.
- Assists Director with economic development projects as needed.
- Collects and analyzes data related to zoning, land use, and economic development activities.
- Prepares Plan Commission, Zoning Board of Appeals, and Historic Preservation Committee agendas.
- Serves as customer service contact person for zoning and other related inquiries
- Prepares professional staff reports as well as written correspondence with the public, as directed by the City Administrator.
- Administers all duties related to the Zoning Board of Appeals.
- Interprets and drafts zoning and subdivision regulations.

Qualifications:

Bachelor's degree in Urban or Regional Planning with emphasis in land use planning or related field; one to three years experience in zoning and planning; experience with GIS desirable; a combination or equivalent experience and/or education may be considered.

More Resources

- *The Zoning of America: Euclid v. Ambler*, by Michael Allan Wolf
- Form-Based Codes Institute, www.formbasedcodes.org
- Zoning Matters, www.zoningmatters.org
- Denver's New Zoning Code, www.newcodedenver.org

Environmental Planner

Some bemoan them as a hurdle in the development process; others celebrate them for protecting natural resources. Like them or not, environmental planning laws are a major part of modern urban planning. As such, the field of environmental planning has seen dramatic growth over the last three decades. Federal laws like the National Environmental Protection Act, the Endangered Species Act, the Clean Water Act and many more state and local statutes largely dictate what is and is not appropriate in the realm of land use, and understanding how they impact planning will be an increasingly important part of any planner's job.

Like many other types of planners, environmental planners work on general and long range plans for their communities, and help to review and approve proposed developments. But they do those tasks through the lens of the environment, focusing specifically on how those plans or projects will impact the environment and how negative impacts can be avoided. Their work revolves around land conservation, environmental protection, hazard mitigation, land surveying, and compliance with environmental regulations.

Stormwater and air quality are major issues in many cities, and are likely to be an element of any environmental planner's work. And as concerns about global warming and carbon emissions grow, there will be an increasing demand for policies and plans that recognize how land use contributes to those problems. Energy efficiency, alternative energy, and green building (in particular, the U.S. Green Building Council's LEED criteria) are emerging as standards in the built environment, and community members are going to expect to see those principles reflected in the work of planners.

To achieve these goals, environmental planners typically work beyond the borders of their city or municipality. They frequently interact with state and federal officials to ensure compliance with a wide range of standards. Environmental planners also work with land trusts, environmental groups and conservationists to secure land for preservation and expand green space.

Though many environmental planning positions will be within municipalities or metropolitan planning organizations, there is a growing number of private consultancies that focus solely on environmental planning issues. These firms manage and prepare environmental documents such as environmental impact reports, initial studies, mitigation reports and a variety of specific environmental analyses.

The specialized tasks require a detailed knowledge base relating to environmental science. Most people working in environmental planning will have some background in science, whether it is a formal degree or just some course work.

Environmental planners address a wide variety of issues and perform a broad array of work. A versatile skill set coupled with scientific specialization will help anyone interested in the field of environmental planning stand out. The ability to learn as you go – and keep up with a rapidly changing set of rules, issues and technologies – will only open more doors.

Bill Broderick

Regional Planner, Denver Regional Council of Governments

Planetizen: *Tell us a little bit about your job.*

BB: I work for a regional planning commission. They have a regional council of governments, and I currently am working on a couple of environmental projects. Although as these projects wax and wane, the lion's share of the work that I do is supporting the regional planning program here. We do a long-range employment and population forecasting process.

We also do a land use planning program, and that's pretty much a vision-based planning process. That's where we try to establish a set of principles and policies for local governments and we try to maintain an environmental aspect to all that, as we look at future land development.

We're concerned about protecting air and water quality, parks and open space, and biodiversity. So that work is sort of an ongoing program I've been involved in. A lot of it's based on where needs have arisen, where local governments have identified problems, areas of concern and then importantly, how we can fund those programs. So a lot of these are grant-based activities.

I'm currently working on a FEMA-funded Natural Hazards Mitigation Plan. The state is funding these with FEMA money and so we're writing this plan for our metropolitan region, which contains roughly nine counties and 52 cities. The state sees this as a way of getting the job done with one contract, and the Natural Hazards Mitigation Plan fits pretty well with our overall mission

as a regional planning commission, so we actually are doing an update of a plan we did five years ago.

That was when the federal government decided that these sorts of plans were a good thing and they sponsored regions and cities and counties individually to write these plans. Plans identify a series of goals for protecting property and life, and so these are part of comprehensive plans in some communities and they're also part of more of the emergency management work for other communities.

Planetizen: *How is your work different from the work another environmental planner would be doing somewhere else in the country?*

BB: It's a pretty specific type of work but it's really perfect for an environmental planner, and that's just one of the projects that environmental planners do. The other activity we have here is a water quality planning program, so that's pretty classic environmental planning. But it's of an urban orientation, because we're in the infrastructure planning for transportation – our agency also does transportation planning – a lot of that sits pretty well with waste water treatment planning.

Planetizen: Environmental planning can be thought of as a combination of land use knowledge and scientific knowledge. How much of each is necessary to do this work?

BB: It depends on the project, but a lot of this stuff is 50/50. Most people in my profession have got a pretty broad background. You either worked for federal agencies like I did, and then you end up working for a city or a county, which is completely different.

I took courses in natural resources as an undergrad, and my graduate work was in public administration and planning. So I think you really need to have a pretty diverse background, as much as you can.

That's what seems to have suited me. You don't want to get too specialized. You delve into engineering in this line of work, but it's mostly public administration in the capacity that most planning is done, not so much engineering. But you do have to have some familiarity with engineering concepts.

Planetizen: What advice would you give someone considering entering the field of environmental planning?

BB: I guess I'd just say that a broad range of experience, whether it's paid or unpaid internships, whatever, would be a good thing unless you know exactly what it is you want to do and it's a good fit for you. I would try to get a fairly broad background for these sorts of things because you never end up doing just one thing all the time. When we look at applicants, we try to find people that can adapt pretty well, and you can see that in people that don't even have work experience, just the coursework they've done or what they're doing in grad school.

Some Significant Employers *(in alphabetical order)*

Bureau of Land Management, www.blm.gov

ESA, www.esassoc.com

Parsons Brinckerhoff, www.pbworld.com

RGP Planning and Development Services, www.rgpcorp.com

SWCA Environmental Consultants, www.swca.com

Sample Job Description

Job Title: Environmental Planner
Job Type: Planning
Date Posted: 07/14/2009
Organization: O2 Planning + Design Inc.
URL: www.o2design.com

Located in Calgary, Alberta, O2 Planning + Design Inc. (O2) is an award-winning firm of landscape architects, land-use analysts, and environmental designers and planners. Founded in 1991, the firm specializes in regional planning and environmental design of rapidly changing and highly valued landscapes. O2 is presently recruiting for the position of Environmental Planner to perform writing, analysis, and project management for a variety of interdisciplinary landscape and regional planning topics, including watershed management, landscape ecology, land use / land cover change, parks and protected areas, and ecosystem goods and services.

Competencies

The ideal candidate will have excellent writing and communication skills, good scientific background in landscape ecology and/or water resources, and an understanding of land use policy and planning concepts. The candidate will have a strong sense of commitment, a willingness to learn more and a desire to work in a dynamic, deadline driven team environment.

Education Requirements

The candidate will have an interdisciplinary graduate degree in Environmental Science, Planning, or Resource Management (M.Sc. preferred), along with an undergraduate degree in a related topic.

Lifestyle

Calgary is a major metropolitan area with a modern, attractive downtown set on the scenic Bow River with views of the Rocky Mountains. Its population is just over a million with 80% of residents living within the City. Calgary boasts one of the sunniest climates in Canada with low rainfall and Chinook winds that bring mild days in winter. Skiing, hiking and camping destinations in Kananaskis Provincial Park and Banff National Park are just one hour from downtown Calgary.

More Resources

- National Environmental Policy Act (NEPA), www.epa.gov/Compliance/nepa
- California Environmental Quality Act (CEQA), ceres.ca.gov/ceqa/more/faq.html
- Environmental Justice Resource Center's Programs, www.ejrc.cau.edu/programs.htm
- Lincoln Institute of Land Policy, www.lincolninst.edu
- National Resources Defense Council, www.nrdc.org/smartgrowth

Public Health Planner

When the idea of land use planning came about, it wasn't just to take control over how cities should look. It was actually inspired by the idea of public health. Putting a coal refinery next to an elementary school was not exactly a healthy choice – and city officials recognized that. So they developed the concept of zoning to keep incompatible uses like these away from each other.

Nowadays, the concept of public health means much more than keeping factories away from schoolchildren. More than just responding to conditions that are likely unhealthy, public health planners are increasingly focusing on improving urban design to encourage more healthy lifestyles. Walkability, access to open space, and proximity to basic goods and services are some of the general concerns of the public health planner. Their job is to work with policy makers and designers to implement those principles. Increasingly, both planners and public health officials are recognizing the importance of patterns of development and urban design in establishing healthy communities.

For the most part, jobs in the field of public health planning are likely to be at the state or federal level. These governmental entities have departments focused specifically on ensuring and improving the equitable health of citizens, and are linked with organizations dedicated specifically to health care issues. Making the connection between health care and land use is still relatively new, as most planners probably think of themselves as being separate from the realm of public health. Part of bridging that gap is communication of the interrelated aspects of land use and health, and many planners entering this field will likely face the task of communicating this relationship to stakeholders, clients and the public at large.

Many jobs in the field of public health planning tend to lean more towards the "public health" side than the "planning" side. Typical job descriptions call for applicants experienced in public health, with degrees in public health, and with a specific knowledge of how disease spreads. Many jobs will deal specifically with making sure a community can respond to outbreaks and health emergencies. From earthquake response to flu outbreaks, public health planners are often involved in making the cities and communities are ready for those worst-case scenarios.

That being said, the role of the urban planner in public health is evolving, and there are many opportunities to integrate sound land use and development in ways that push forward public health agendae. Emerging information has revealed that siting homes and schools within certain distances of highways leads to increased incidences of health issues like asthma. And neighborhoods that have no sidewalk infrastructure or little access to fresh foods tend to have higer rates of obesity. As these connections between land use and real health issues become more prevalent, policies will begin to take shape to avoid the unhealthy mistakes of the past. Whether it's insituting enlightened zoning rules or buiding safer intersections, urban planning is increasingly responding to issues of public health.

And as those issues become more widely known and widely experienced, the need for planners with a knowledge of health impacts will become much greater. They'll be needed to review and understand why communities are unhealthy and translate those realities into public policies that promote healthier lifestyles. Public health planners will be key players in creating cities that are both safe and healthy.

Dee Merriam

Community Planner, Centers for Disease Control and Prevention

Planetizen: Describe a typical day in your job.

DM: There are no typical days. In a nutshell, my job is to try to translate planning to the public health folks that I'm working with here. I also translate public health opportunities to planning and design professionals.

I do quite a few presentations, but I also get to work on project reviews. I've done reviews for LEED-ND. I'm working on sustainable community guides for local government, which are under development. I read articles and make recommendations on them. I've also gotten to do some of my own independent research.

Planetizen: What do you like best about your job?

DM: Working in public health gives you credibility, when you walk in the door, that you don't have as a designer or a planner. When you're a planner, you're seen as being the hack with the developer or you're from the government and local government. Folks don't really, necessarily, give you the credibility. So, that instant credibility when I walk in the room is very, very pleasant.

Planetizen: What challenges do you face?

DM: Not having a formal public health background. I've only been in CDC for about a year and a half, so I'm having to learn a lot of the public health terminology. In my experience, every type of organization and different places have different keywords that you can win the argument with. So, it takes

a little time to figure out how to frame your issues.

Planetizen: How is what you do at CDC different from what another planner working in public health may be doing?

DM: I'm probably much more research-focused. I'm also much more interested in trying to figure out the strategies. I guess, the difference is – having worked in local, state and Federal governments now – they all have very different ways that they accomplish what they accomplish. So, I think, the big difference is between working at the Federal level versus working at the local level.

Many of the local health departments are

considered to be part of the local government. An opportunity there is for them to forge personal relationships between the planning and design professionals in their community. And how to bring the health rationale and the health argument for why we need sidewalks and why we need connectivity. Why we need the kinds of things that we're trying to do to design places that promote healthy lifestyles.

Planetizen: If you were to talk to someone who's interested in pursuing a career in public health planning, what advice would you offer them?

DM: To be open to it. And that it is something that is definitely burgeoning. As we all are aware, public health was the foundation for planning. The enabling legislation was based on past public health issues. I believe over the last 60 or 70 years, we've gotten away from acknowledging that as being the basic foundation of what we're trying to accomplish. It has weakened some of our positions. We need to go back and look a lot harder at those public health foundations.

One of the things we're doing here at CDC, of course, is trying the evidence-based rationale behind why we do what we do. And I think that only strengthens what we're trying to do as planners and designers. It makes us much more effective, instead of doing just what we think is good or what looks good, aesthetically, to us. We have validated information on which we're basing those decisions.

Some Significant Employers *(in alphabetical order)*

AARP Livable Communities, www.aarp.org/research/ppi/liv-com

American Red Cross, www.redcross.org

Centers for Disease Control and Prevention, www.cdc.gov/employment
Human Resources: 770.488.1725

Federal Emergency Management Agency, www.fema.gov

Kaiser Permanente, www.kaiserpermanentejobs.org

National Institutes of Health, www.jobs.nih.gov

United Way, www.liveunited.org/jobs

Sample Job Description

Job Title: Public Health Educator
Job Type: Planning
Date Posted: 03/31/2009
Organization: Bureau of Chronic Disease Control, City of New York
URL: www.nyc.gov/html/doh/home.html

The Public Health Educator will exhibit skills and high comfort level in instructing and organizing other adults; experience conducting field work in low-income neighborhoods; knowledge of physical activity, early childhood development, coordination and management techniques; and a highly developed ability to implement culturally relevant programs that address physical activity in low-income New York City neighborhoods. The position involves extensive field work in communities and outreach with other public and private agencies and community organizations in order to increase physical activity among children in low-income communities.

Duties include, but are not limited to:
- Preparing for and conducting presentations and workshops for daycare, pre-kindergarten and elementary school teachers and staff on a standardized physical activity and nutrition curriculum that is designed to address childhood obesity.
- Establishing and/or maintaining collaborative relationships with child care centers (including daycares and elementary schools) in communities across New York City.
- Working with local communities to organize physical activity trainings, including identifying and recruiting interested staff
- Providing outreach, technical assistance and feedback to trained daycare and elementary school staff; and implementing evaluation strategies in the field.
- Conducting field work to assess community needs and to increase opportunities for physical activity via community education and training.
- Providing onsite technical assistance to child care staff on implementing physical activity in their classrooms; and attending regular meetings and providing updates as appropriate regarding effectiveness of interventions and field investigations.

Preferred Skills:
Experience working with children. Experience working in the field, specifically in low-income settings. Experience working in a team environment. Excellent interpersonal and communications skills. Knowledge of nutrition and public health, including health behavior change strategies.

More Resources

- American Planning Association, Planning and Community Health Research Center, www.planning.org/nationalcenters/health
- Centers for Disease Control and Prevention, Emergency Preparedness and Response, www.bt.cdc.gov/planning
- Urban Sprawl and Public Health, Howard Frumkin, Lawrence Frank, Richard Jackson, 2004, Island Press

Consultant

A "planning consultant" is less a particular type of job and more like a giant umbrella covering a wide variety of backgrounds, professions and employers. That umbrella covers anyone working in the non-public sector and performing part of the planning process in a land use context.

Consultants include everything from comprehensive, global firms like HNTB, Parsons Brinkerhoff, and Arup that handle every aspect of building, engineering and planning to independent contractors like George Osner, who does work-for-hire as an urban and environmental planner.

Mid-level consulting firms often specialize to stand out, covering niches such as bike and pedestrian planning, form-based codes, or smart growth. Working in a consultancy often involves doing the same work a planner would do – creating land use plans, consulting building codes, working with neighborhood groups – with the added dimension of the work being for a client.

"I'm one of those people who I don't think could ever work in the public sector, because I'd be too focused on one geography," says Scott Page, founder of Interface Studio (profiled on pg. 48). "And as someone with attention deficit disorder, as I often think I have, I really enjoy getting to know new places. Getting to work in a new neighborhood, a new city, doing that investigative work, getting to know the people who live there and then helping them solve their problems is really satisfying."

Two growing sectors in planning consulting are economic research and community engagement. Over the past several years, bringing the community into the decision-making process has become more and more important and viewed as a necessary alternative to a history of top-down planning. Consulting firms like the National Charrette Institute teach community engagement, while others specialize in leading the engagement process from start to finish.

And as cities across the country have faced severe budget shortfalls, city planning services are being contracted out entirely. In early 2009, the city council of Petaluma, California voted to eliminate the entire planning department and contract services out to a private consulting firm. The wave of the future might be considerable growth in the private sector.

But it is much more likely as a planning consultant that you'll be working on the real estate development side of the equation. Architects and developers often need someone on their team who can speak "plannerese" and help manage the city planning department's processes.

The options are still endless – consultants manage feasability studies, land conservation, stadium siting, write design guidelines, specific plans, you name it.

David Wenzel, AICP, LEED

National Chairman of Urban Design and Planning, HNTB

Planetizen: Tell me how your career path evolved. How did you get to where you're at now?

DW: The University of Cincinnati had a very rigorous urban design and planning program, and I was fascinated, at the time, with the concept of sustainability. I think sustainability was one of those concepts that planners got many, many years before other disciplines – how to design with nature, as opposed to against nature. I went through that program and became very interested in the land use and policy planning side of things. When I graduated, I came to work with HNTB and started their planning practice here.

Then I wanted to get into the public sector, so I went to the City of Dallas, and was the Chief Land Use Planner, and was then promoted to be the Assistant Planning Director. Then I was the community development director for a suburb of Denver. Then I wanted to return to the private sector, and about 15 years ago came back to HNTB.

Planetizen: What do you see as the main difference between working in the public and private sectors?

DW: I think they're both very stimulating areas to work in. In the private sector, you probably have more variety in your diet, so to speak, a wider array of project types that you're involved in. In the public sector, though, I think one of the real benefits is the ability to stay engaged in a project, and become part of the implementation of that project. That tends to be a little more difficult on the private planning side, that you're somebody who is brought in to problem

solve for that client, and then the client is the one who implements that solution. I find them both to be very satisfying and intriguing sides of the planning profession.

Planetizen: Along that same line, what do you see as the challenges and the rewards of your work?

DW: Probably one of the biggest challenges is the fact that there's not a right answer. You are relying upon your technical skills to come up with the best approaches, but that's a real challenge. Because, again, it's not like designing a roadway, where there's certain standards. It's going to be so many inches thick, and the lanes are going to be so wide. Land use planning, in particular, is somewhat subjective.

But, by the same token, I think that's one of the greatest opportunities and greatest rewards is that it is a problem-solving exercise. When you are able to develop a solution with others, and convince the client, or the general public, of the merits of that – that's an extremely satisfying accomplishment.

Planetizen: What types of attributes and personality would make one a good planner in the private sector?

DW: I think there are a couple that I can think of, right off the top. Since I've grown older, I've really started to acknowledge and recognize people with these skill sets. One of them, in particular, is the ability to be naturally inquisitive. What I mean by that is problem solving, being able to pose questions, not in a threatening way, but pose questions in a very interested way. I find that to be a very unique skill set that not a lot of people have.

A second skill set that I would say is very important for a planner is the ability to listen. The ability to, again, work with others, and to hear from others what they're thinking. Not to go in with preconceived notions.

Another useful skill set is the ability to come up with technical solutions based upon some very sound principles. I'd say those would be the three.

Planetizen: What advice would you give to someone interested in becoming a planning consultant?

DW: They should really seek out the opportunity to either work or observe, for a little bit of time, the different sectors of planning. The private sector, the public sector, as well as the different dimensions within those. There are environmental planners, there are land use planners, there are transportation planners.

My advice would be to really be very open for a while in your career, to exploring these different dimensions of planning, and different settings for planning in the public and private sector.

Some Significant Employers *(in alphabetical order)*

This is just a small sample of the thousands of planning consultant groups out there. Each of these sites has a careers page listing job openings.

Arup, www.arup.com

Calthorpe Associates, www.calthorpe.com

Fregonese Associates, www.frego.com

HNTB, www.hntb.com

HOK, www.hok.com

MIG, Inc., www.migcom.com

Wallace, Roberts and Todd, www.wrtdesign.com

Sample Job Description

Job Title: Real Estate Market Analyst/Urban Planner
Job Type: Planning
Date Posted: 09/04/2009
Organization: RKG Associates, Inc.
URL: www.rkg1.com

RKG Associates, Inc. is a leading national consulting firm providing economic, planning, and real estate advisory services to a wide variety of public and private clients throughout the United States. RKG is looking to hire a person in its Alexandria, VA office with knowledge and interest in urban and regional planning, urban redevelopment, economic development, and real estate development. Alexandria is one of America's finest mid-size cities.

Project opportunities include:
- Financial feasibility and market analysis,
- Regional demographic and economic analysis, implementation strategies,
- Downtown revitalization, waterfront revitalization, military base reuse,
- Economic & Fiscal Impact Analysis: Fiscal and economic impact analysis.

The candidate must be proficient at statistical analysis and possess an understanding of: regional economic analysis, development proformas, real estate market research, and fiscal impact analysis. Proficiency with MS Excel, MS Word, and basic knowledge of MS Access and PowerPoint are required. A working knowledge of ArcGIS and its applications is also desirable.

Qualifications:
The ideal candidate will have a minimum of a Masters degree with a concentration in real estate, urban studies, planning, business, or urban economics. Candidates should have one to three years experience in planning, real estate, or related profession. Candidate must possess: (1) sound computer and technical skills, (2) good organization skills, (3) effective written and verbal communication skills, (4) problem-solving skills, and (5) the ability to work effectively in small groups The position is full-time and available immediately. RKG Associates offers a competitive salary and benefits package. Salary is commensurate with experience and includes the potential for semi-annual bonuses and future advancement for the right candidate.

More Resources

- Planetizen's Consultants Directory, www.planetizen.com/consultants
- American Planning Association Consultants Directory, www.planning.org/consultants

Preservationist

History can be hard to define, but for cities, much of history is rooted in the built environment. Preserving that history means preserving the buildings that tell the story of a place. This is the realm of historic preservation.

But to say that preservationists are simply caretakers of aging buildings oversimplifies the profession. Preservationists and conservationists are people who document the history of places and buildings, highlight their significance, and utilize planning and architectural strategies to maintain that significance for future generations. Though specialists, historic preservationists tend to wear many hats. They have to be researchers, communicators and architectural generalists. They need to understand how preservation laws dictate certain processes within a community, the historic resources in that community the law is intended to protect, and the various stakeholders who are affected by those laws.

Increasingly, preservation is also being seen as the environmentally-friendly option. By preserving existing buildings, developers and cities can reduce the waste and energy use required to construct new properties – and at the same time preserve some of the historic character of a place.

There are a few ways of becoming a historic preservationist. One is to approach it from an architectural background. Knowledge of architecture is incredibly important to preservation, as it is typically buildings that are the focus of a preservationists day-to-day work. An educational background in architecture is a leg-up, but is by no means a pre-requisite. There are many ways to acquire knowledge of architectural forms and history without entering a formal university program.

Another way people become preservationists is simply out of need. There are hardly any places out there without historic resources. Because these resources need to be managed and preserved, someone within the municipal government (or through a private consultancy) is likely to take the reins. If no specialist is present, somebody will probably be asked to become that specialist. This is especially true in smaller towns. Larger towns and cities often have their own historic resources office.

The third way people enter the field of preservation is from the citizen's standpoint. Many cities have preservation commissions that report to city councils, and these boards are typically filled with citizens. It is often the mere existence of an interest in history or architecture that might push someone onto one of these commissions.

The day-to-day work of a historic preservation planner has a strong research focus, often requiring them to dig up old documents and facts about historic properties to find out the best way to intervene and perform preservation. But it also requires a lot of work in the field, visiting sites and assessing their needs. The field may also require a bit of advocacy, as it is often the preservationists who have to prove to city officials or developers that the structures they're planning to demolish actually do have historic value to the community. Sometimes, this can be the trickiest part of the job.

Broad knowledge of history and architecture are crucial tools for historic preservation planners, and will make the job of preserving the built history a more intuitive task. The most important tool to have is a passion for the history of cities – and a recognition of the importance it has in their futures.

Hector Abreu-Cintron
Acrhitectural Conservator, Historic Preservation Services

Planetizen: What do you like best about what you do?

HAC: I've always had an incredible passion for protection and the saving of our legacy; meaning the legacy of our history as a people. I see, in this case, historic buildings as evidence of our past. Keeping those things alive and visible for future generations is an amazing responsibility. It is so unknown by people. Some people think, well what's preservation? What's the importance? Then I ask, "When you go on vacation, when you go to Paris, where do you go? Do you go to a Wal-Mart? No. You go to the Eiffel Tower. You go to the Arc de Triomphe. You go to Notre Dame. You go to the historic buildings. When we go places, the first places we want to see are the historic towns, to go downtown and see the historic districts and the museums. It's so much a part of our lives that we take it for granted. I guess, that's what I love doing. It's in knowing that I've hopefully contributed to keeping these buildings and resources around for longer so that people in the future can look at these and enjoy them just as I am enjoying them now.

Planetizen: What are some of the challenges you face in your work?

HAC: Some of the biggest challenges I faced were trying to convince people who are not preservationists why this is important. That's extremely challenging, not only at the federal level but at the state level, in the local community, and with mayors. I have had discussions with city officials, local communities, city council members, and it's amazing that some people still don't get it. I would think that at this point, most of us

would get it, but then I have to realize that not everyone is into preservation. There are still people out there who think progress, modern, and new is the way to go. That's a huge challenge, just trying to educate. That's number one for me – trying to just educate people that this is important. This is something that should be done. It's not just to make things look pretty. Another challenge has been, I would say, the lack of respect that the field has had in the past. It doesn't have much now, and it's still fighting to get it. There's been a lack of the understanding that this is profession. It's been thought of as being like a hobby or something you do just to spend the time. It's not. This is a full-fledged profession. You work at this; you get paid to do this.

Planetizen: Describe a typical day in your job.

HAC: A typical day is I wake up, check my emails, then start working. It depends. Other times, I'm in the library, or I'm in the archives doing research. Then I can gather that all together, and sit at the computer, and just start writing. So, a lot of it is collecting data, going to do research, and then coming back to the office, just kind of collecting data. But, sometimes it's also trying to get a heads-up on other projects, trying to find other stuff out there that could be useful.

Planetizen: What advice would you offer someone considering entering the field?

HAC: First of all, and I always tell my students this, it's real life. First, do you want to get rich doing this? And if they say yes, I say well then you're in the wrong field. You can make a decent living and if you're very good you can make a fairly nice living. But if you're in this for the money, then you don't have the right mindset. The other thing is that it's a very people-oriented field. It's not a very introverted field. It's extremely extroverted. If you're very introverted, you're very shy, you don't like to talk to people it's not a very good field. It's the kind of field where you're out there. You're doing public meetings, you're meeting with the community, you're meeting with mayors, you're meeting with office directors, you're meeting with planners, you're meeting with architects. You've got to make your case. It's an extremely extroverted field. So, it's not for the shy. So, the economics plays a role, and so does the social aspect. This is, I think, a very important field in our social history. Preservation has changed. It used to be that people think that it's only about restoring buildings. But now I think preservation, particularly through the planning field, has become an extremely important aspect of every community's planning process. It's integral to the social betterment of the community.

Some Significant Employers *(in alphabetical order)*

Advisory Council on Historic Preservation, www.achp.gov

Engineering and Environment, Inc., www.eeiinfo.com

Florida Trust for Historic Preservation, www.floridatrust.org

HDR, www.hdrinc.com

Mead & Hunt, Inc., www.meadhunt.com

National Trust for Historic Preservation, www.preservationnation.org

New Mexico Historic Preservation Division, www.nmhistoricpreservation.org

Ohio Historic Preservation Office, www.ohiohistory.org

Preservation Action, www.preservationaction.org

Preservation Delaware, www.preservationde.org

San Antonio Conservation Society, www.saconservation.org

Southeastern Archaeological Research, Inc. (SEARCH), http://searchinc.com

Sample Job Description

Job Title: Historic Preservation and Outreach Planner
Job Type: Planning
Date Posted: 11/02/2009
Organization: The Maryland-National Capital Park and Planning Commission
URL: www.mncppc.org/jobs

The Historic Preservation and Outreach Planner position will support the Montgomery County Historic Preservation Commission (HPC) and the Historic Preservation Section through the implementation of the "Education and Outreach Plan for Historic Preservation."

The selected individual will plan and implement educational outreach programs and materials to promote the HPC and historic preservation in Montgomery County; provide support for the County Executive Award for Historic Preservation programs; and coordinate and administer the Historic Preservation Grant fund. The incumbent may also assist with the identification and evaluation of resources for listing in the Master Plan for Historic Preservation and with the review of Historic Area Work Permits

This position may be filled at the Planner or Senior Planner level.

Minimum Qualifications:
Senior Planner:
Master's degree in planning, architecture, parks, engineering, environmental science, or equivalent disciplines related to the job function and one (1) year of progressively responsible professional level planning experience; OR an equivalent combination of education and experience.

Planner:
Bachelor's degree in planning, architecture, parks, engineering, environmental science, or related subjects and one (1) year of professional planning experience; or an equivalent combination of education and experience.

Supplemental Information:
Strong technical writing and presentation skills are essential, as are excellent computer skills, including use of desktop and presentation software.

Local travel throughout Montgomery County and elsewhere in Maryland is required. Attendance at evening and/or weekend meetings approximately two (2) times per month is required.

More Resources

- National Trust for Historic Preservation, www.preservationnation.org
- American Cultural Resources Association, www.acra-crm.org
- Preservation Directory, www.preservationdirectory.com
- *Historic Preservation: An Introduction to Its History, Principles, and Practice*, by Norman Tyler

GIS Administrator

Geographic information systems (GIS) are becoming an essential tool in almost every planning organization. From cities to private consultancies to environmental firms, GIS is being used by planners to understand and analyze spatial data of all sorts. As the amount of spatial data increases, the need for people able to use and understand the information will become even more important.

Spatial information about such planning-related topics as zoning, parcel maps, transportation systems and housing enable planners to model and comprehend the areas they're planning, and to take educated guesses about what the future might hold for these places. Using the information requires some technical familiarity, but you don't need to be a computer genius to work with GIS. Oftentimes, GIS specialists come into their positions from a geography background. This formal background gives them an understanding of how information can explain geographic features – from geology to hydrology to housing density. But others come into GIS from a purely technical background. Typical job postings for GIS positions request (in addition to GIS experience) an educational background in computer science or related areas. Some even require a specific educational background in GIS, which some planning programs provide. That being said, a willingness to learn GIS will often be enough to land yourself in a GIS-role in a smaller organization, though this is much more likely after you've already been working there.

Working in GIS often means working on a wide variety of data sets. Especially within cities, GIS specialists will typically be in charge of organizing and updating the spatial information for many city departments. However, planning departments tend to be the main users of such spatial data. Planning departments typically use GIS for mapping, modeling and analysis, and this type of spatial data use is increasingly a part of comprehensive planning efforts.

On a day-to-day basis, GIS specialists will work on the collection, creation and manipulation of spatial data. The most effective GIS professionals not only understand how to use the software, but also how to perform the types of data analysis that support the goals of the planning department or firm. Having an understanding about how planners use data is seen as a very valuable skill in a GIS specialist.

There is some concern amongst planners that becoming familiar with technologies like GIS will pigeonhole them into being "GIS person." This attitude is slowly changing. In the past (and even today) technical people have been tasked with much of the computer-related work – from GIS to information technology to website maintenance. But as planners and the workforce in general becomes more tech-savvy and computer-literate, the division between the "technical person" and the rest of the organization will fade away.

As is the case in many aspects of the planning world, the broader your knowledge base the better. It's highly likely that GIS will only become more ubiquitous in the planning world. Whether you want to think of this in terms of being a valuable asset to the community you serve or simply in terms of job security, GIS represents an increasingly important part of urban planning.

Jennifer Higgs

GIS Manager, Metropolitan Government of Nashville & Davidson County, TN

Planetizen: You are a GIS manager, but do you also have a planning background?

JH: I don't know that anybody on our GIS team has a planning background. It just happens to be that the main staff for GIS is in the planning department for the county. And that's because planning has been the big proponent and user of GIS.

Planetizen: Because you work so closely with the planning department, would you consider yourself a planner?

JH: No. I assist the planners. We do analysis for them. We probably help most with showing what's coming up and what's being done around the city. What's going on in the current planning-type stuff, where applications are coming in and the location of those applications. That's where we have the most impact within the web of what's going on in the county.

Then we do analysis-type stuff for community planning. For design, we've helped planners with some 3D analysis. We're not really ever asked to help make the decisions in that respect. I still consider myself a GIS professional who happens to work in the planning department. We're running the GIS for pretty much most all of the departments. We manage the database. We don't do all the editing of the data but we make sure they're all available for everybody. We do application development, web design and stuff like that.

Planetizen: On a day-to-day basis, how much GIS work is there?

JH: There's four of us in this department

that are just busy all day long. And every department has people that use GIS. Just about every planner in this agency has it on their desktop and uses it everyday.

Planetizen: Describe a typical day working with the planning department.

JH: We recently worked on projects for site locations. I'm doing a project that's looking at tax districts, doing analysis for that. Something different comes up every day that somebody needs.

We do analysis for zoning ordinances or tax amendments that are being proposed. There was one proposed recently for allowing people to have chickens and we were looking at the criteria and determining who would be able to have chickens if that went through. We have people doing that kind of analysis. We have a person who does analysis about where you can put a liquor store.

I do a lot of programming. There's two of us that do a lot of programming and web development. A lot of my day is spent improving on our current websites or coming up with new ideas and working on new stuff to release. We just have a lot of day-to-day administration and making sure the database is up, making sure users can get access, troubleshooting people's calls when they are having issues. It's a big hodgepodge of stuff that we are doing every day just depending on what is needed.

Planetizen: How important would you say knowledge about planning would be to someone trying to work with GIS?

JH: For GIS itself, I don't know that it's so important. It's important if you're helping the planning department with GIS. But not necessarily. I don't need to know anything about planning – I need to know what question are they trying to answer and what data does it take to try to answer that question. But I may know nothing about whether that is a good way to design or what the implications are going to be of that decision. It's almost better not to know that, not to have a preconceived idea of what the answer should be.

We come at it from the point of not having a preconceived idea. You give us what you want, what the question is, and we'll take the appropriate data and give you an answer. You may not like the answer, but there's the answer.

I don't know that a knowledge of planning is that important. But it has helped me to become more important to the agency, because I know what everybody does and how they work together and what's going on here and there. So as far as keeping your career, or keeping your position, it's important. As far as actually doing the analysis, knowing the data sets that we have is more important, I think.

Planetizen: What advice would you give someone interested in pursuing a career in the GIS profession?

JH: Learn programming. Everybody likes somebody who can maybe not be able do major application development, but be able to write something that will do a job faster or customize something. People will say "I want something that does this but not exactly that." And that's probably been what helped me the most is that I did have that understanding and I keep learning new things as they come out. I delve in and learn the new technology. So I think that getting your hand on that, taking extra classes, doing online stuff, even if you haven't done it before. Not everybody is suited towards doing that, but even if you're out looking for samples that you can implement that other people have written, and can help other people implement those things. You've got to be innovative and you have to take initiative.

Some Significant Employers *(in alphabetical order)*

Avencia Incorporated, www.avencia.com

Environmental Systems Research Institute, Inc. (ESRI), http://careers.esri.com

Michael Baker Corporation, www.mbakercorp.com

Wiser Company, LLC, www.wiserco.com

Sample Job Description

Job Title: GIS Specialist
Job Type: Planning
Date Posted: 03/25/2009
Organization: Jefferson City, MO
URL: www.jeffcitymo.org

The City of Jefferson City, Mo has a unique opportunity for the right person. This is an advanced professional, technical, and consultative position. Jefferson City is in need of either an ArcSDE Administrator with Microsoft SQL Server experience or an ArcGIS Server Web Programmer/Administrator. If you can do both, or are willing to learn the other skill then you are the perfect candidate.

Education and/or experience for either track:

- Bachelor's degree in Geography, Computer Science, Planning, or closely related field
- Three years GIS experience with at least two years at Technician or Analyst level
- Thorough knowledge of the principles, best practices, terminology and trends in GIS
- Responsible individual with the ability to work independently
- Prior municipal GIS experience preferred
- Ability to obtain valid MO Drivers License

- Acceptable background check

Track 1 – ArcSDE Administrator: Knowledge, Skills, and Abilities

- Experience in automating ArcSDE processes.
- Experience administering ArcSDE geodatabases in a multi user, versioned, replicated, enterprise, environment.
- Experience in geodatabase design
- Experience with Microsoft SQL Server 2005

Track 2 – ArcGIS Server Web Programmer/Administrator: Knowledge, Skills, and Abilities

- Experience in ArcGIS Server web development using VB.net
- Programming: VB.net, JavaScript, asp.net, FLEX or Silverlight
- Experience in Managing ArcGIS Server, its components, and its architecture
- Experience in administering ArcIMS websites

More Resources

- The Urban and Regional Information Systems Association, www.urisa.org
- GIS Careers, www.giscareers.com
- GIS.com, www.gis.com

Land Use Lawyer

The body of law pertaining to land use is extensive and specific, ranging from easements and variances to nuisance and eminent domain laws. The fifth edition of *The American Way of Zoning* by Patricia E. Salkin, for example, fills five volumes. So it is no wonder that a subset of attorneys specializing in land use law has become a necessary part of many planning processes, particularly ones of significant size.

Land use attorneys are most often employed by developers, or law firms with a real estate specialty. But Lora A. Lucero, AICP, Esq., says, "It is much larger than that. Land use and planning law encompasses decisions made at the federal, state and local levels about how we use our limited natural resources for the present and future generations. It's not simply private development we're concerned about, but public investments and decisions regarding transportation and other important community resources that influence the timing and location of private development decisions."

Cellular telephone companies and utilities are also likely to have a land use attorney on staff, due to the high number of issues that arise in regards to citing towers or power stations.

Of course, being an attorney requires a law degree. Choosing this career path means three years of law school and passing your state's bar exam. There are also many programs where you can get a joint degree, such as The University of Kansas' program that leads to a Master of Urban Planning and a J.D. degree of the School of Law, which is a four-year program.

A specific focus on land use is not exactly necessary from the start, but as you move through your law education and even you first years of practice, you may find the field to be not only interesting but also very active. Land use regulations, interest groups, competing developers, and ever-changing local ordinances make much of the planning process a legally-binded endeavor.

As laws, environmental standards, and local policies shift and become more stringent, the need for capable and quick-thinking land use lawyers will become much greater. No developer will even think about building something as minor as a parking spot without a knowledgeable land use lawyer on hand. Being able to navigate the intricacies of the legal system as it pertains to development requires a deep understanding of the benefits and drawbacks of land use. Maintaining and growing that understanding will create a very valuable set of assets for any attorney considering the field of land use law.

Cecily Talbert Barclay

Partner, Bingham McCutchen

Planetizen: Tell us about your career path. How did you get to where you are today?

CB: I've always been interested in real property and development. I worked for a couple of years after college, then went to law school. I took real property courses, which I very much enjoyed. I started working as a real estate attorney for two years. Then the early '90s recession hit San Francisco and I spent a lot of time doing insolvency work, but often with a heavy orientation towards real estate.

When I say real estate I don't just mean the "transactions of the dirt," but how projects were affecting communities during that downturn, coming up with solutions and problems with respect to leases, infrastructure that was half built in communities and that sort of thing. Then, as the economy rebounded in 1996, I officially moved over to a full-time land use practice.

I was mentored by a terrific group of attorneys in our firm, particularly a partner of mine, Dan Curtin, who is often referred to as the 'dean of land use' in California. Dan had published a book called *Curtin's Californian Planning and Land Use Law.* I coauthored that book with him for close to 10 years and I now author the book on my own.

Planetizen: What is your typical day?

CB: My day is divided between serving my clients and their projects and working with the attorneys in our law firm. I probably spend an average of two to three hours a day just managing the practice and the people that I work with. The rest of the time is spent working on my clients projects.

Then I'm usually on conference calls and in meetings all day long from nine o'clock in the morning until five o'clock in the evening. If I have city council meetings I'm only at meetings until midnight. It is very typical in today's world to be sending hundreds of emails a day, or at least dozens, and then being on conference calls that could go back-to-back all day long with a meeting or two buttressed in between.

Generally, I probably have two client meetings a day. Those are typically with city staff and consultants, EIR consultants, geologist, engineers, city attorneys and public relations folks. Where I've gotten to in my career now after being an attorney for 21 years is, I do a lot of strategic planning and legal advice at the same time. My job is to let people understand what the laws are, but then also help make decisions on how to move forward.

Planetizen: What do you find most challenging about your work?

CB: The challenges are explaining it to people what you actually do! Particularly to clients who are new to the development business. Part of the challenge is really getting your future clients and your current clients to understand how to best utilize you and how you can add value to their project. I think a current challenge is that for the last ten years our economy has needed to have land use attorneys to help get projects to market that had a lot of complexity to them, and frankly a lot of challenges by local neighbors or NIMBYs, as we call them.

Planetizen: What advice would you give someone who is interested in becoming a land use attorney?

CB: I would advise them to take courses and get real world experience in real estate transactional. This is the time, when you're starting, to understand how people buy and sell property, how you borrow money, how you get title insurance, and to understand easements. Really get the legal aspects of owning real estate down and do that early, because it'll be a lot harder to do that later.

Similarly, you should try to get some litigation experience. Understand the legal process, what it is like to actually draft a complaint or have to file an answer and do some discovery and write a brief. Because one of the interesting things about land use law is that you have to be both a real estate attorney and a litigator as well as a land use attorney.

Some Significant Employers *(in alphabetical order)*

Bingham McCutchen LLP, www.bingham.com

Duane Morris LLP, www.duanemorris.com

Edwards Angell Palmer & Dodge LLP, www.eapdlaw.com

Foley & Lardner LLP, www.foley.com

Fulbright & Jaworski, LLP, www.fulbright.com/realestate

Greenberg Traurig, P.A., www.gtlaw.com

Husch Blackwell Sanders LLP, www.huschblackwell.com

Jones Day, www.jonesday.com

McGlinchey-Stafford, PLLC, www.mcglinchey.com

Skadden, Arps, Slate, Meagher & Flom LLP, www.skadden.com

The Spagnuolo Group, www.bcrealestatelawyers.com

Squire, Sanders & Dempsey L.L.P., www.ssd.com

Sample Job Description

Job Title: Real Estate Attorney
Job Type: Planning
Date Posted: 11/09/2009
Organization: Community Health Systems Professional Services Corporation
URL: www.chs.net/career_openings/corporate.html

Tennessee real estate attorney with broad commercial experience representing buyers, sellers, developers, borrowers/lenders, landlords and tenants sought for Senior Counsel position with Community Health Systems Professional Services Corporation. The successful candidate will have 5-7 years of the indicated real estate experience with a major Nashville law firm. Prior representation of national clients is required; healthcare experience is a bonus. The successful candidate will report directly to the General Counsel and will work directly and independently with the Acquisitions Department, the Real Estate Department, and individual hospital clients.

Job Description/Requirements:
- Attorney will directly handle all aspects of commercial real estate transactions, from letter of intent stage, through the negotiation phase, due diligence, closing, and preparation of closing binders.
- Types of transactions will include: undeveloped land transactions, development of hospital and other healthcare projects (new and expansion), hospital transactions (buy/sell), and leasing (both sides).
- Attorney will review and address title and survey issues, zoning issues, resolution of encumbrance and restriction issues, environmental and other due diligence issues that arise in transactions.
- Attorney will draft and negotiate the real estate documents for all transaction types, including ongoing development of form agreements for use by hospital clients.
- Attorney must be able to work on multiple transactions simultaneously, be well-organized, and be able to work independently (both regarding supervision and required support assistance).
- Top academic credentials from a top law school required. Tennessee law licence in good standing required. Some travel required for due diligence and closings.

More Resources

- American Bar Association's Section of State and Local Government Law
  www.abanet.org/statelocal
- Patricia Salkin's blog, Law of the Land, lawoftheland.wordpress.com
- Journal of Land Use and Environmental Law, www.law.fsu.edu/journals/landuse

Design

Livermore Village, by Opticos Design and Architecture

In the not-too-distant past, architecture and urban planning were seen as very distinct disciplines. As concern has grown for over the state of the built environment, new areas of practice have developed to fill in the perceived gap between the two. Today, the areas of urban practice involving design have grown significantly. Urban designers range from architects with an urbanist bent to creative types that use the language of design to communicate social and demographic information.

To be involved in urban issues from a design standpoint, one needs to be creative and flexible. There is an artistic aspect, certainly, but it must be balanced with the ability to be holistic and change tack for a client or the public. Unlike a fine artist, an architect and designer is responsible for a permanent fixture that will become part of the framework of everyday life.

Landscape architecture, previously viewed as mostly horticultural, now concerns itself with many of the same issues that urban planners consider. Some of those issues include accessibility, wayfinding, and that illusive quality that makes attractive public spaces. In fact, an entire new area called 'landscape urbanism' has been created by landscape architects who assert that their role is paramount in the creation of public spaces.

As people have become more design-savvy, the role of design in planning has expanded considerably. At the same time, the economic downturn means fewer projects. If you're interested in this field, now may be a good time to develop your skills.

Urban Designer

Urban design is a relatively new area of practice and is still somewhat ill-defined. But that lack of definition makes it an exciting place to be, as urban designers push the boundaries around how the language of design can create solutions to urban issues.

Scott Page, an urban designer in Philadelphia (profiled on the next page) says that urban design is actually investigative work. "It's about really scratching below the surface," says Page. "Getting to know the people that live there, what's happened in the past. And helping them to solve some of their problems."

In the past, urban design was exclusive to architects who found they were more interested in the spaces between buildings. Today, it is no longer necessary to have a degree in architecture – but it helps, because the bias is still in place. Urban design programs vary for this very reason. Some are one-year intensives for architects, others are incorporated in a master of urban planning degree. If you're applying for school with an interest in urban design, it would behoove you to confirm that the school you're applying to has a studio element.

Patternbooks and design guidelines are a common product for an urban designer. Designers survey the look and feel of a city or town's neighborhoods, talk to residents about the elements of their city that they like, and create a guide for developers and architects that captures the essence of those design elements.

In fact, public participation has become a central differentiating factor between architecture and urban design. The "charrette," an antique French term for a sort of quick design exercise for architecture students, has evolved into a popular way of engaging today's communities in a public process. Using nothing more than giant pads of paper and markerboards, urban designers use their expertise to communicate the desires of the public for their built environment. Through the language of design, the public process is shortened considerably and consensus is built. As Jane Jacobs oberved, "Design is people."

Computer-aided design (CAD) has become a dominant tool in urban design, ranging from the hardcore architectural tool AutoCAD to the considerably simpler SketchUp. Photoshop is even used to cut-and-paste elements of a cityscape over underdeveloped or blighted landscapes to illustrate possibilities. But the ability to draw is still a useful, in-demand skill. Hand-drawn sketches, scaled plans, diagrams, maps, etc., are all tools of the urban designer's trade.

Urban planner Kevin Lynch opened up another niche in urban design in 1960 with his book *The Image of the City*. Lynch talked about the "legibility" of a city, or the ease with which people can find their way around. Wayfinding and environmental graphic design spring from those ideas, and a handful of firms focusing on signage and clarity of urban spaces have resulted.

And as in all aspects of urban planning at the turn of the 21st century, sustainability is on everyone's radar. Urban design today is focusing on green design ideas like incorporating agriculture in cities, managing stormwater through permeable surfaces, and other methods for lessening the impact of development.

Scott Page

Principal, Interface Studio

Planetizen: Tell us about your career path.

SP: The initial goal, going into undergraduate, was to be an architect. And that came from exposure I had to architecture classes in high school. And I just assumed that was something that I was going to do. It was actually my year in Paris that changed my mind. As I realized that I was, actually, really interested in the larger urban issues and design, but I had very little patience for drawing details.

I ended up taking a year off, after I got back from Paris, and then went to school for planning at University of Pennsylvania, which is where I figured that planning would hit a lot of the interests that I really had, both the larger interests about how cities function, how you can begin to have some influence on how cities are shaped and evolve over time. But I still very much had an interest in taking the design skills I learned from architecture, but applying them to the planning profession. And that's where urban design found me, more or less.

My first job was working on the 1996 Olympics in Atlanta. I was working for a small design firm, based out of Boston. They had a team to put together some urban design strategies for specific corridors within Atlanta.

Planetizen: What does a typical day look like in your job?

SP: I have a small office of seven people, total. So, I spend a good part of my day

talking with each of the people in my office about the projects that they're working on, the information they're collecting, and what they're learning about the places that they're working.

I'm also spending a lot of time with clients. I'm still, at this point, the primary contact for most of our clients, on our projects. Frequently I'm organizing public meetings, slowly leaking ideas that we have to convince clients that they're the right thing to do. So, it's a lot of people management. I think it would be very hard for me to do the kind of urban design work that this firm does without being very good on the people end. Because, ultimately, we're trying to sell our ideas. But, we're also selling our ideas in thecontext of what our clients would like to see.

Planetizen: What do you find most challenging about being an urban designer?

SP: for me, one of the things that's really challenging is managing all of the different agendas. In the old days, when you had Kings, or Robert Moses, or, at least in Philadelphia that would be Ed Bacon, there was a lot of top-down direction. And now we have foundations that have an agenda, bankers that have an agenda, community groups that have an agenda, city agencies that have agendas, all of them. Not all of those agendas are always synched, or in line with one another. So, that's one of the more challenging things – understanding what each main player at the table is really interested in, and then finding a way to channel that interest towards a common goal.

Planetizen: What advice would you give someone interested in being an urban designer?

SP: I had some professors at Penn who would tell me, flat out, you can't be an urban designer unless you have an architecture background. And I never agreed with that. I still don't agree with it. In fact, I'm the only person in my office with an architecture background. Everyone else comes from very different places. And that's a good thing.

But, what I would suggest for someone going into the profession is that they need to go to some type of creative program, even if it's for only a year. So, whether it's architecture, or landscape architecture, or graphic design, or fine arts, something of that nature, for a few semesters, is immensely helpful.

And it's not just to help on the graphic end, it also helps on the thinking end. Because you can go through an analysis and collect all of the data that you need. At some point, you have to take a leap. And when you take that leap, you have to be comfortable doing it. And I think a design program helps you gain that comfort level, and make that kind of decision that you can't just glean from the analysis.

Some Significant Employers *(in alphabetical order)*

CityWorks, www.cityworks.biz

Moore Iacofano Goltsman (MIG), www.migcom.com

Schreiber Anderson Associates, www.saa-madison.com

Space Syntax, www.spacesyntax.com

Urban Design Associates, www.urbandesignassociates.com

Urban Strategies, www.urbanstrategies.com

Sample Job Description

Job Title: Urban Designer
Job Type: Design
Date Posted: 01/29/2009
Organization: Ekistics Town Planning
URL: www.ekistics.ca

Ekistics requires an urban designer to enhance its professional team. This position will work collaboratively as part of a multi-disciplinary design group on projects throughout British Columbia, as well as internationally.

Reporting to a Principal, the Urban Designer's responsibilities include:

- Complex urban design and development planning;
- Developing community visions;
- Preparing urban design guidelines and reports;
- Facilitating public consultation, presentations and coordinating with clients, municipalities, consultants and agencies; and
- Managing projects and guiding professional staff.

The preferred candidate will possess the following skills and abilities:

- A university degree in physical design (architecture, landscape architecture, urban design).
- A post graduate degree with a focus on urban design or equivalent professional experience of three to five years in urban design and development planning.
- Membership or eligibility for membership in the British Columbia Society of Landscape Architects and the Canadian Institute of Planners is preferred.
- A good understanding of land development issues, community planning and local government procedures.
- Working knowledge of Microsoft Office, Adobe Creative Suite and CAD. Ability to work in a professional, high-pressure team environment.
- Excellent command, written and spoken, of the English language; and,
- Excellent interpersonal skills.

More Resources

- Resource for Urban Design Information, www.rudi.net
- UC Berkeley College of Environmental Design www.lib.berkeley.edu/ENVI/design_ada.php
- Congress for New Urbanism, www.cnu.org
- Web Urban Design, www.weburbandesign.com
- Terreform, www.terreform.org

Landscape Architect

When planners talk about what they do, they often refer to the "built environment." This tends to be accurate, with buildings and infrastructure making up much of the work. But in the spaces between buildings or on the edges, the environment is not built at all. Green space and landscaping is common around new projects, be they offices, housing or retail. There are even full plots of land dedicated to green space (also known as parks). Planners are involved in creating these spaces, but it is often landscape architects who ultimately guide their design.

Many planning firms have in-house landscape architects. In this context, landscape architects use their background in land forms and environmental design to help guide planning, site layout and project aesthetics. While landscape architects are usually involved in a wide variety of projects, they are also the guiding force behind highly pastoral projects like new parks, gardens, cemeteries and waterfront developments. Like an architect, design and artistic ability are also helpful skills. "It is not about just dressing something that the architect gives us," says John Loomis, principal at SWA. "We would always like to be in there right at the same time the architect starts on the project, if possible."

Landscape architects are typically people who have studied landscape architecture, but a formal education is not necessary to perform the work of one. What is needed is a knowledge of land forms, plants, environmental conditions and a geologic sense of time. Unlike buildings, landscapes are largely predefined based on geography, and are subject to the rules of nature. Understanding these rules is essential to anyone working on landscape architecture.

Landscape architects are also involved with restoration and preservation projects, working to revitalize natural areas that have been negatively impacted by human development.

Like planning, the fruits of landscape architecture take time to ripen. Because the medium is often plantlife, it may take years for the project to grow into the desired vision. Thinking long-term about projects is another essential tool for a landscape architect.

But the field is much more than pretty gardens and sculpted shrubbery. The rise of the environmental movement and the almost parallel resurgence of urban living has many city dwellers seeking a connection to nature and natural elements in their highly human-made urban environs. Indeed, some within the field have even argued that landscape architecture has a more important impact on urban development than architecture. The emerging field of landscape urbanism expands the dynamic and growth-based aspects of landscape architecture to the realm of urban development. Organic growth and environmentally-conscious planning are havily emphasized. In this light, landscape architects are becoming some of the most progressive urban theorists today.

From planning and designing entire new parks to picking the right plantings for a freeway embankment, the work of a landscape architect is highly varied. Some firms focus on only a specific kind of project, but landscape architects early in their career should be prepared to work on a broad range of projects. As the appreciation of natural elements increases and the desire for more and better parks and open spaces grows, landscape architecture is likely to become an even more important part of the development of cities.

R. Umashankar

Landscape Architecture Consultant, RUNG Design

Planetizen: What was your first job once you finished your master's in landscape architecture?

RU: For the first few years, I came out at a time when the economy wasn't doing too well, and my first job actually ended up being that of an architect in a small firm in Columbia, Missouri. I went back to my initial training as an architect, and I just worked on that for almost three years, after which I found a job as more of a physical planner. That's when I really started to use some of my capabilities as a landscape architect. That's the beauty of the profession is that people don't fully comprehend what all landscape architects do, when it ranges all the way from planning a city to planning gardens.

Planetizen: Describe a typical day at your job.

RU: A typical day for me would be a lot of managing communication, managing process and products. Working with a smaller team, I typically am working with a team of two or three people when it comes to a planning effort. I'm typically managing the clientele, recommending decisions. So you've got this whole series of things that you've got to manage, making sure everything belongs in the right place so that ten years from now they're not thinking, "Why did they put that there?"

So maybe you spend half a day just sitting at a desk and scribbling away on sheets of paper that, at the end of the day, look like they're meaningless. It just like your thought process just expressed with a pen. Then you're guiding somebody. So you give that person a sketch. Then they take it and come back to you with a formal sketch or solution. And you sit down with them to understand what

they did and offer them some critique and some suggestions on what they could do to make it better. If it's good then you say OK, lets finalize it. That's when the process of producing begins.

Planetizen: What do you like best about working as a landscape architect?

RU: For me it's the gratification of having helped a higher education institution. I think it's something that you grow to be fond of. The goal of a higher education institution is, in part, to educate us. They have a purpose to themselves. You feel like you have helped with a greater cause. When you help them make the good decision, when you help them at times save money, which can amount to millions of dollars, you feel good because you worked hard at that process.

I'll go back to some places five years after I've worked on a master plan and say look, they did it just the way we told them to. You would not have had a part in how they built the project. But you told them things to consider. As a campus planner, and in most of the planning world, you're not producing a tangible product which is going to be built tomorrow. You're making recommendations.

So you've left the college for almost half a decade and you come back and you see that they've done pretty much what you told them. It's like, number one, you get the extra confidence that you were right about your recommendation. Then you feel good that they actually listened to you.

Planetizen: What advice would you give someone who was interested in entering the landscape architecture field?

RU: I would tell them that the profession is very broad. There are many options into what you can choose to do within the profession. Landscape architecture is basically an umbrella that gives you the ability to get into a whole host of different things. Be prepared to work hard; it doesn't pay well to begin with. When you start off, you can't expect to do too well for yourself, and that's just the norm in the industry. But it's challenging and it does give you some unique opportunities. And it's a very fulfilling profession. It's a very gratifying profession. And there is a lot of variety to it.

Planetizen: If you were to start your career over today, what, if anything, would you do differently?

RU: If I were to start my career over, with the exception of having spent maybe a couple of years working as an architect right out of college – which is a couple of years that I think I lost – I probably would not have changed much. One thing I would do, and I see the value of doing is to be active in the networks that you create right from the day you get into school, is be active, be pro-active, be visible, because that is an essential part of a profession such as ours.

And you can't be shy. You've got to be out there. You've got to be speaking – you've got to talk. You've got to be speaking your ideas. You've got to be getting to know your peers. You've got to be getting to know who are the people who are the leaders in the profession; try to understand how they work and what they do. So I suggest staying active from day one outside of what is just happening in your school and in your program.

Some Significant Employers *(in alphabetical order)*

AECOM, www.aecom.com

BWM Group, www.bwmgrp.com

Hargreaves Associates, www.hargreaves.com

Land Strategies, Inc., www.landstrategiesinc.com

Sasaki Associates, Inc., www.sasaki.com

SWA Group, www.swagroup.com

TBG Partners, www.tbg-inc.com

Wallace Roberts & Todd, www.wrtdesign.com

Sample Job Description

Job Title: Strategic Planner / Landscape Architect
Job Type: Design
Date Posted: 05/20/2009
Organization: Environmental Planning & Design, LLC
URL: www.epd-pgh.com

Environmental Planning and Design, LLC (EPD) is hiring an experienced Senior Strategic Planner. Applicants should be familiar with the Pennsylvania Municipalities Planning Code. Candidates will assist Principals in developing community master plans; subdivision and land development plans; comprehensive plans; zoning ordinances and strategic plans; facilitating public meetings; manage GIS; writing proposals and grants; completing technical research; and other duties as required with minimal supervision. The position requires excellent verbal and written skills, and proficiency in computer programs such as Microsoft Excel and ArcGIS. AICP registration is required.

EPD is also hiring a Senior Landscape Architect with 10 years of experience to manage large-scale construction projects. The Landscape Architect will work on a wide array of public and private-sector projects in urban design, riverfront design, and construction documentation. Candidates must be able to handle a fast-paced and energetic environment. Must be a registered Landscape Architect; computer skills are a must: Microstation or AutoCAD, Microsoft Excel, etc.

EPD was established in 1939 to provide public and private clients community planning, landscape architectural, urban design services. Our 70 years of experience has allowed us to develop a nationally acclaimed practice. EPD's projects are diverse and include: municipal and community planning; strategic planning; recreational planning and development; commercial development; residential planning and development projects.

Education Requirements: Bachelors or Masters in Urban Planning and/or, Regional Planning; Bachelors or Masters in Landscape Architecture.

More Resources

- American Society of Landscape Architects, www.asla.org
- Canadian Society of Landscape Architects, http://csla.ca
- International Federation of Landscape Architects, www.iflaonline.org
- Library of American Landscape History, www.lalh.org

Architect

Including "architect" in this book is kind of like including "surgeon" in a book about general practitioners. An architect is in many ways a specialist, concerned with the engineering, infrastructure and design feats involved in creating buildings. However, like the careers included here, architects are interested in how people use the built environment and are key in the process of what gets built.

It is often said that planners are interested in the space between the buildings, while architects are focused on the buildings themselves. This is somewhat unfair, because architects are also involved in planning the non-building areas of the lot, and often work directly with city planners on incorporating the building into the existing streetscape.

An architect is also called upon to have a high level of technical expertise, because they will be working directly with the structural, mechanical, and electrical engineers who will be making their renderings a reality. They need to understand building codes, local and federal building requirements, and have an intimate knowledge of building materials and how they behave.

Daniel Parolek, founding principal of Opticos Design and Architecture, says that architects use many different skill sets as they perform their job. "My daily tasks range from very business-oriented tasks such as communication with clients, project supervision, quality control and proposal creation, to the more design-oriented tasks such as sketching design alternatives to hand off to project managers and drawing and watercoloring perspective drawings. I always make sure not to stop doing the fun aspects as part of my job."

As in some other careers in planning,

architects began to create specializations in order to carve out a niche in a competitive business. Specializations include health care, resorts, public housing, and the growing field of green building.

Becoming a registered architect requires significantly more education than most of the careers we've profiled. Unlike most four-year undergraduate programs, a bachelor of architecture is five years long and requires a great deal of studio instruction. If you have already received a B.S. or B.A. in another discipline, you can attend a two-to-three year Master of Architecture I program. Post-college, most states require that graduates complete three years of internship with an architectural firm. And finally, applicants must pass the Architect Registration Examination (ARE) in order to practice in the field.

If you're considering a career in architecture, architect David Baker of david baker + partners says, "Do it. This is a great field. You get to be creative, you get to do stuff and make stuff. Architects create physical things that they can see, that interact with people and make people happy or sad. You get to make an impact and an impression. It has its ups and downs – you might want to be prepared for a more durable second career, like a short-order cook or a dental hygienist, because architecture is expensive, and there's not always money. But architects are happy, satisfied people."

Today, sustainability is a growing concern within the field, and a growing area of business. Concerns over the impact of global warming are changing the materials and methods of building. If you're considering a career in architecture, you would do well to focus on sustainable practices.

Steve Mouzon

Principal, Mouzon Design and the New Urban Guild

Planetizen: What was your career path?

SM: The first firm I worked in was a firm in my hometown of Huntsville, Alabama. My wife and I bought a lot in 1984 and started building what was going to be a completely self-sufficient homestead. But the problem was, because of what a normal architect salary was, I was spending so much time working to pay the mortgage that we never had time to properly do all the raising of chickens, and garden, and all this sort of thing. I was working every available moment for the next several years just to pay for the house.

I opened my own firm in 1991. By this time, we were a fairly decent-sized firm and doing a lot of local work, stuff within 50 miles. But there was one fellow, Nathan Norris, who I met at my very first Seaside event.

He at the time was what they called a town manager at a place called Gorham's Bluff in north Alabama that was really strapped for cash. He told me, "We know we've got to replan the town." He said, "Granted, you have no town planning experience yourself, but all the things you're saying are in the right place. I know your architectural work." He said, "What we'll do, we'll gamble on you if you will work for dirt. In other words, we'll give you a couple of lots, then we'll let you replan Gorham's Bluff."

That seemed like a good step in the right direction for me, so I did that. I'm still town architect there. Then one thing led to another, and by early 2002 DPZ [Duany Plater-Zyberk Associates] was coming to Huntsville to do the Village of Providence. That's the name of the development there.

So I decided, well, these guys have been my heroes since the early '80s, so I'll just volunteer a week at a time and see what happens. I did, and we really hit it off, and I've been doing consulting work with them ever since. We've worked with all sorts of wonderful clients that we would have never had have the opportunity to otherwise.

But one little caveat I ought to throw in there before I get to the end of this monologue, and that is that, basically, in the last 10 years, there have been very few things in really none of the last seven that I've done for which I am qualified.

In other words, these are all things that I'm making up as I go along in that it's all self-appointed stuff. In good New Urbanist fashion, I just say hey, I think this needs to be done. So I go out and try it. Sometimes we succeed; sometimes we don't. But we try it anyway.

Planetizen: What advice would you give to someone who is looking at school now, interested in becoming an architect, and interested in creating change?

SM: I would tell them that they are probably about the luckiest of the architecture students of the last generation or so, precisely because of the fact that they don't have a snowball's chance of getting a job right now.

What that will do – everybody goes through a time like this once or twice in a career when there's a really bone-jarring recession. This arguably is the worst one for architecture and construction since the Great Depression. Looking back on it, I don't think it'll be remembered as everybody's Great Depression, but it could well be remembered that way for architecture and construction.

What that means is, of all the points in life at which you could hang on to your ideals while flipping burgers or doing something else to actually buy groceries, the students and the recent graduates are the ones who are the best-equipped to do that. Because they haven't got sucked into the machine yet and have all these financial commitments and this sort of thing that would force them to leave and go to another profession.

Instead, they can actually be sitting there and doing much of what I've been doing for last several years anyway, and that is advancing ideas and initiatives to which there's no money attached at the moment, but which could help establish them – well, at least own the road to being an authority on these things.

Planetizen: What are the challenges and rewards of working as an architect?

If you're in a normal firm, then, as bleak as this sounds, in my opinion, the challenges and the risks far outweigh the benefits. Working as a normal architect, where you do the regular projects you get on a local scale. Because most architects, quite frankly, if they care anything about design but aren't one of the stars, then most of them will probably die penniless. It's just a fact of our profession. There are two ways out of it: either become an international celebrity and make ridiculously large fees, which is wonderful for those few people; or treat it purely as a money-making venture with no ideals and no beliefs, so you don't get sidetracked into ideals. Then you can make a decent profit and retire at a normal age.

But if you go about it, on the other hand, seeking how to innovate, in the way that a lot of New Urbanists do, then it's one of the most gratifying things that I can imagine.

Some Significant Employers *(in alphabetical order)*

Duany Plater-Zyberk Associates, www.dpz.com

Gensler, www.gensler.com

HDR, www.hdrinc.com

HOK, www.hok.com

Skidmore Owings & Merrill LLP, www.som.com

URS Corporation, www.urscorp.com

Sample Job Description

Job Title: Architect
Job Type: Design
Date Posted: 3/11/2009
Organization: Russo Development/Hackensack, NJ
URL: www.russodevelopment.com

Russo Development, LLC located in Hackensack, NJ is seeking a Project Architect to join our architecture department.

Required Education: Bachelor/Master's Degree in Architecture.

Experience: Minimum seven (7) years, full time, construction document preparation or job captain level responsibilities on projects exceeding 10 million dollars.

Primary Job Responsibilities: Working within our architectural staff on the following architectural functions for various multifamily residential, commercial, office and industrial projects in our development pipeline:

- Preparation of master plans and design proposals for new projects for large-scale redevelopment projects;
- Preparation of conceptual and schematic design documents including elevations and 3-D renderings;
- Preparation of construction documents to be used for permitting, bidding and construction including floor plans, sections, details, reflected ceiling plans, interior elevations, and basic M/E/P drawings such as underground plumbing, power plans, and lighting plans;
- Interaction with Russo's in-house civil engineering team;
- Interaction with Russo's outside design consultants including structural, M/E/P, and geotechnical on the engineering design of all projects; and
- Work with Russo's in-house construction management crew on various construction administration tasks including shop drawing review, project inspections, client meetings, and contractor interaction.

Secondary Job Responsibilities: Prepare design documents for renovations within Russo's existing building portfolio in collaboration with the Property Management and Leasing Departments.

More Resources

- American Institute of Architects, www.aia.org
- The Architectural Record, http://archrecord.construction.com
- *A Pattern Language,* Christopher Alexander
- The Architect's Newspaper, www.archpaper.com
- *Becoming an Architect: A Guide to Careers in Design,* by Len Waldrep

Development

Daybreak is a master-plannned community outside of Salt Lake City, with streets lined with porch-fronted homes.

When it comes to what gets built, development is the catalyst. Not to say that money drives everything (as we'll see in the area of non-profit development), but the driving impulse for what gets built happens primarily through the development field. Planners, architects and urban designers are in many ways just reacting to the initial act of a developer looking at a piece of land and seeing possibility.

Magic Johnson is a case in point. The former pro basketball player turned a desire to help African-American neighborhoods escape from poverty into a booming development company, with an unusual hybrid of for-profit and non-profit interests. He saw potential in ethnic communities that many developers shied away from, and used his celebrity as a way to attract investment.

Because developers are intimately involved with the money side of the equation, they're also the closest to the actual costs of construction. Juggling expenses while still making a high-quality product is a tricky game, and good developers learn where they can skimp and where they have to shell out the big bucks. The construction business itself is notoriously corrupt and geared towards cranking out a limited number of home styles for efficiency's sake, so developers have their hands full when trying to make attractive places.

To the urban planning-educated, the world of development can seem a bit difficult to crack. Hopefully we can help shed some light on the field, because the career options are clearly engaging to those interested in the built environment.

For-Profit Developer

A for-profit developer is a person or a company that builds developments – be they residential, retail, office, industrial, or some combination thereof – with the goal of earning a profit in the end. Developers range from solo entrepreneurs to giant development firms like Transwestern.

Some developers also manage their properties, keeping tenants happy and spaces filled.

Don Monti, president and CEO of Renaissance Downtowns, LLC, says that his average day "starts early and ends late. It's a combination of putting out fires. It's a combination of dealing with day-to-day development decisions, and it's keeping an organization humming in a very difficult time."

With the downturn in the economy, the development business is significantly slower than in the past. Many developers are sitting on development opportunities until they see how the dust settles on property value and growth in the retail sector. Others are channeling their energies in new directions.

"The suburbanization of America is over," said Morgan Dene Oliver, CEO of OliverMcMillan, at an Urban Land Institute conference. "Infill development is going to be an important evolution as our economy changes. And it's going to be good business. When the spigot turns back on, it's going to be funding infill projects."

And that spigot likely will turn back on. As many in the real estate workd can testify, development comes in waves, with building booms and busting bubbles. Accepting the fact that there will be dry periods as well as floods is a mental hill to climb. But once that realization is made, enlightened developers will sleep much more soundly at night.

One of the drawbacks of working in development is the lack of a steady paycheck. According to Salary.com, 80 percent of developers work on commission, making it a tough business to get into without some sort of nest egg. But the risks of the business eventually pay off for most developers, earning $100,000 and up after a few years.

So, this is not a field for the easily scared. The field of for-profit development is highly competitive, and developers need to stay alert and ready for any opportunity to pounce before someone else can. This might call to mind some greasy, backstabbing crook just looking to make an easy buck, but that's hardly the world of development. Increasingly, developers are finding that going for the easy buck often leaves a lot of opportunity behind. Consumers and occupants are demanding more and more from their built environment – from access to transit to environmental awareness to coherence with surrounding aesthetics. Simply building projects that will be profitable ignores the whole market sector of people who want quality places to live, work and play. And this market sector is growing.

Coming to the world of development from an urban planning background will be a major step up in this area. With its emphasis on improving communities based on local desires, urban planning and its ideals are finding their way into real estate development. It's likely that this trend will continue, as a growing number of people steadily take more interest in the urban development around them. Being open to the concerns and desires of the public is a cornerstone of planning, and it's becoming one of real estate. As that trend continues, the real estate developers who are receptive to those needs will likely be building the best and most successful projects.

Seth Brown

Principal, Aspen Equities, LLC

Planetizen: Tell us what you do as a developer.

SB: I orchestrate an entire development project from selecting a site, finding investors, working with an architect to developing plans, or planners if need be for larger projects, engineers, picking general contractors, overseeing construction, and actually completing the project, seeing it out and selling it. So it's really the entire thing from receiving a project, overseeing a project, and completing it.

Planetizen: What was your career path?

SB: There's a particular course at Yale called "Study of the City," taught by Alex Garvin. He's been teaching the class for over 35 years. I think it's a somewhat rare undergraduate course on basically, planning and development that essentially consists of a number of development-related role-playing games.

And it really gives you a flavor, as much as possible, in a class, of what development is like, what big planning decisions are like and what it's like to be in the rough-and-tumble world of development, politics, and all of those things. So, I think that initially inspired me to start thinking about development as a career. And as an undergrad I interned for the Trammell Crow Companies in Denver. I think that was my first development job.

After I finished my undergraduate degree, I went to work for a management consulting firm and gained some experience in the business world, but still knew that I really was more interested in cities and development. So after a year or two, I went to work for a mid-sized developer based in Brooklyn

called The Hudson Companies. That was my first real development job, and I started as a junior project manager working on a couple of 100-unit projects in Manhattan, and I started getting some experience.

Planetizen: Do you have a personal approach to development?

SB: My projects all have a pretty substantial green focus. I care a lot about design and trying to add something to the neighborhoods I work in. But for me, the challenge is how to do something worthwhile, interesting, and in neighborhoods that people appreciate. Improve the urban fabric, and also is green and also in profitable. If you don't have that, you're not going to be a developer for too long.

Planetizen: What do you like best about your current position and what do you feel is most challenging?

SB: What I like best is that there are a lot of different parts of working on a development project. You interact with architects and engineers. There's the whole design side of things. You interact with the finance community and try to figure out, "How do I entice investors to work on my project, to invest in my project? How do I get lenders or banks to lend on my project?" You're working with the city. You're trying to get permits. There's sometimes, on big projects, a political aspect to it. It involves a lot of different areas, which makes it interesting.

I find it really interesting to try to put together deals and sort of create the idea, like, what is this project? What could it be? Who should be involved in it? What would make it most appealing as a development project, whether it's a rental building or condos or commercial property?

What I find less appealing, after a certain amount of time, is actually running the project. Which, obviously, if you're building a building, it doesn't happen that quickly. You might work on a single project for two, three, four, five years. And at a certain point, it becomes sort of tiresome.

Planetizen: What advice would you give to someone interested in working in development?

SB: You can gain experience on the planning and architecture side or the finance side or the construction side. Those are all really useful. I think that the primary skill that you really need is really understanding how a project gets financed and being credible in that respect, because you're not going to do anything if you can't convince lenders and investors to work with you.

Some Significant Employers *(in alphabetical order)*

Armada/Hoffler Development Company, www.armadahoffler.com

Bluegreen Communities, www.bluegreencommunities.com

CPC Group, www.cpcgroup.gg

DMB Associates, Inc., www.dmbinc.com

Hines Interests Limited Partnership, www.hines.com

Lauth Property Group, www.lauth.net

National Realty and Development Corp., www.nrdc.com

Opus Corporation, www.opuscorp.com

The Related Companies, www.related.com

The Richard E. Jacobs Group, LLC, www.rejacobsgroup.com

The Shorenstein Company, www.shorenstein.com

Trammell Crow Company, www.trammellcrow.com

Transwestern, www.transwestern.net

Sample Job Description

Job Title: Real Estate Services Assistant
Job Type: Development
Date Posted: 11/11/2009
Organization: CB Richard Ellis Group, Inc.
URL: www.cbre.com

Our Asset Services group transforms assets into opportunities by providing measurable results in property management, leasing, tenant relations, project and construction management, technical services, risk management, purchasing, energy management and financial reporting.

Responsibilities

- Provide full administrative support including phone support, typing, reports, filing and distribution of correspondence.
- Schedule and coordinate meetings/special events as requested.
- Assist in lease administration activities including lease set up, administer lease changes, generate reports, etc.
- Prepare and coordinate bid proposals and service contracts and approved invoices.
- Assist in bidding process and ensure compliance with Playbook and National initiatives for these bids.
- Ensure prompt completion of PM Data warehouse (PMDW).
- Maintain lease and property files.
- Track and file contracts and insurance certificate; maintain follow-up system for expirations.
- Promote and foster positive relationships with tenants and owners and track service calls as required.
- Assist with monthly and quarterly management reports as well as annual budget preparation.
- Prepare A/R status worksheets, initiate late payment calls, reconcile A/R, and follow up on collections as required.

Qualifications

- High school diploma, 1+ years of related experience and/or training.
- Impeccable customer service skills.
- Ability to comprehend instructions, short correspondence, and memos and ask clarifying questions to ensure understanding.
- Superb Organizational Skills.
- Exceptional interpersonal and collaboration abilities.
- Basic knowledge of financial terms and principles.
- Ability to prioritize and adjust to shifting priorities in a fast paced environment.

More Resources

- Urban Land Institute, www.uli.org
- National Commercial Real Estate Developers Assocation, www.naiop.org
- Retail Traffic Magazine, http://retailtrafficmag.com
- RealtyTrac, www.realtytrac.com
- LandThink, www.landthink.com

Non-Profit Developer

Is affordable housing your passion? A lot of people who go into urban planning have a desire to help people in need find places to live. If you want to be directly involved in creating affordable housing, community-based, non-profit real estate development is where you need to be.

Government solutions for affordable housing have been less than effective for the past sixty-odd years. Everyone knows about the urban renewal programs that herded people in poverty into projects isolated from the rest of the city. Government, while well-intentioned, created many of the problems planners are trying to fix today.

Meanwhile, non-profit developers have been steadily establishing new models, using public-private partnerships to help meet the housing needs of low- and moderate-income families. Funding is cobbled together from private donations, HUD programs, and a variety of other sources to make these projects a reality.

Aside from the funding aspect, the development process is no different than a for-profit venture. The developer works on a building from start to finish: acquiring the land, approving the designs, getting permits from the city, sourcing materials, directing the construction, and finally opening the building. Nonprofits are more likely to go all the way though to the management phase, because the goal is to maintain an affordable housing option and not sell units just so they could raise in value with the market.

Increasingly, cities are instituting new zoning rules that require a certain percentage of affordable housing in new housing developments. These inclusionary zoning rules have their detractors, but many within the field of non-profit development are in support of the effort on the part of cities to encourage and mandate affordable housing options.

Of course, there are always local stakeholders who are afraid of their property values declining if an affordable housing project is built in their neighborhood. Assuaging the public and making consessions to residents is part of the development process. In 2007, for example, the Disney Corporation fought a plan to put an apartment building with 255 affordable units within spitting distance of Disneyland in Southern California. These sorts of concerns and power plays are always an obstacle to getting affordable housing built.

Nonprofit developers are often at the forefront of revitalization projects, because they are more willing to take a risk on location than a for-profit developer. They've been particularly engaged with transit-oriented development, a strategy of intensifying development around transit hubs, because residents of affordable housing projects are more likely to need to take transit to get around. "Somebody's got to go first," says Linda Mandolini, executive director of Eden Housing. "Somebody's got to be a catalyst. And oftentimes, the affordable developers can generate certain kinds of funding that the for-profits can't that will help promote these projects."

A degree in urban planning or real estate development is not necessary, but would no doubt be a helpful tool in identifying development opportunities and locating where those projects are most needed. Whether it's the conversion of an old office tower to condominiums or a small-lot infill project, the urban realm is full of opportunities for creative non-profit developers.

Eugene P. Walker, Jr.

President, Mercy Housing Southeast

Planetizen: Could you tell us what Mercy Housing does?

EW: Mercy Housing, Inc. provides safe, quality, affordable housing, all over the country. We're a national nonprofit developer of housing. 'Nonprofit' developer is a little misleading. As a nonprofit entity, you can make profits. The difference is that you don't use those profits to pay shareholders. You use those profits by reinvesting them into whatever specific work that you're trying to do. In this case, it's housing.

We specialize in various types of financing to put together housing for individuals who, in general, make less than the normal median income. We use tax credits and HUD 202 programs to provide housing for people who, in general, make less than 60 to 80 percent of median income.

Planetizen: What, in your job, do you end up doing every day?

EW: My job is several-fold. One part of it is fundraising. So we have resident service programs that we have to raise funds for, and we think that's part of what separates us as a developer.

The first thing you have to do is find a piece of property. And that could either be land or an existing apartment complex or an existing house. And when you find that, you look for an opportunity to finance it in a way that it could be affordable. So, right now, what I primarily focus on is finding new pieces of property and then getting them into our pipeline of development.

The next step in development is to make

sure that it's zoned properly: multi-family or single-family, the right number of units, that type of thing. And then, once we do that, we begin to work on the actual financing, and that's to raise the money to either rehabilitate or construct new properties that will end up being affordable.

And then the next step, after we build the property, we get it financed, and then we actually have to go through the process of building the property. And we, in general, use general contractors to work with us on that. We oversee them as they actually build the properties.

Once the property is complete, we get a certificate of occupancy, and then we can begin to lease units to individuals. Actually, at Mercy, we have a management company that does all the leasing work. So we work through that process in getting individuals to qualify to live in our units. And then we collect rent and try to set up our resident service programs so that people can not only have a great, safe, decent, quality place to live, but also begin to be exposed to something different than they may have been exposed to before.

We find that when you just put someone in a nice place, it's even better if you can provide some type of resident services that will allow them to feel like it's important to keep the place nice and clean and all that. Just having been in affordable housing when I was growing up, I understand why that's important.

Planetizen: What do you like best about working in the field of nonprofit development?

EW: I always tell my staff, I like the beginning. I like when I go out and find a piece of property, or an apartment complex that needs to be rehabilitated and redeveloped. Then I like when it is done. Whether it is newly constructed or rehabilitated, and when I go out and see the people and talk to them after they have moved in and they say, so many of them say, this is the best place I have ever lived, and thank you. That is what I like.

Planetizen: What do you find most challenging?

EW: In the development business, pretty much all of it is hard. Sometimes, politically people don't want it to happen. Sometimes the neighborhood doesn't want the development to happen. Sometimes it is extremely difficult to obtain financing, and the financing has so many different facets; equity to debt, debt service coverage ratios, sources of financing, HUD, grants, loans. So it is just so many different things that have to be in the air. I would guess that just pulling everything together and making it work is what makes it so difficult.

Planetizen: What advice would you give to someone who is interested in going into a career in nonprofit development?

EW: I would recommend that first of all they have a passion for helping people. At the end of the day, that is what you are doing in nonprofit development. You are going to see a lot of other people in the development business that will have the potential to earn a great deal more money. You have to have a passion for helping people.

Some Significant Employers *(in alphabetical order)*

Bridge Housing, www.bridgehousing.com/Employment-Opportunities

EAH Nonprofit Housing, www.eahhousing.org/hr/job-listing.asp

Mercy Housing, http://mercyhousing.ats.hrsmart.com/cgi-bin/a/searchjobs_quick.cgi

National Community Renaissance, www.schdc.org/jobs.htm

The NRP Group, LLC, www.nrpgroup.com/jobopportunities.html

Pennrose Properties, LLC, www.pennrose.com/employment.shtml

Sample Job Description

Job Title: Director of Real Estate Planning and Development
Job Type: Development
Date Posted: 03/31/2009
Organization: Community Works Rhode Island
URL: www.communityworksri.org

Community Works Rhode Island (CWRI) is hiring a Director of Real Estate Planning and Development. CWRI is a community economic development corporation in Providence, RI which provides a comprehensive approach to neighborhood stabilization through investment in mixed-income housing, commercial and community space; facilitation of infrastructure, greenspace and streetscape improvements; sustainable management of its assets; community organizing; and homeownership training and foreclosure counseling. CWRI is a charter affiliate of NeighborWorks America.

The position directs real estate development activities and manages the development of projects, including identification of properties, financial and feasibility analysis, development of budgets and timeframes, creation of architectural designs, securing public/private funds, managing staff, consultants and contractors, monitoring the development, and selling and leasing properties.

Minimum BA/BS degree in architecture, planning, real estate development, community development or related is required. Graduate degree desired.

- Minimum 10 years in affordable, multi-family housing and community development.
- Knowledge of best practices related to multifamily affordable housing, and innovative neighborhood planning and community revitalization techniques.
- Ability to identify viable development opportunities that meet CWRI's mission.
- Expertise in creating a three to five year pipeline of projects, and managing for growth in capacity and production.
- Experience with financing resources for affordable housing such as LIHTC, New Markets, CDBG, HOME, BHRI, FHLB-AHP, historic and energy tax credits.
- Experience creating successful projects on or ahead of schedule, on budget with maximum financial return, highest quality, and greatest community impact.
- Ability to manage a multi-party development team of lawyers, accountants, architects, engineers and investors.
- Experience developing feasibility analyses, create pro formas, monitor project budgets and timelines.
- Expertise in green building, adaptive reuse and historic restoration.

More Resources

- U.S. Dept. of Housing and Urban Development, http://portal.hud.gov
- Housing Partnership Network, www.housingpartnership.net
- *Breaking Ground: A Beginner's Guide For Nonprofit Developers,* from the Federal Reserve Bank of Dallas, www.community-wealth.org/_pdfs/tools/cdcs/tool-breaking-ground.pdf

Economic Developer

In the structure of city government, economic development is an odd bird. Sometimes it is a department within City Hall, or a subset of the planning department. Other times it is an independent entity. Either way, the goal of Economic Development Organizations (EDOs) is the same – to attract business to a city or region, and maintain a healthy business climate.

So how does economic development connect with land use? For one, large corporations can make a significant impact on local economies in terms of jobs and taxes, so economic developers are often looking for ways to accommodate the needs of those corporations when they go looking for a new shipping center or corporate office. EDOs work with businesses to find them attractive properties, and work with city government to create incentives to attract such businesses.

Tension can arise between economic developers and the communities they serve over the attention the development department pays to large corporations over small business within the area. Economic developers can also be accused of taking the side of business over the community. For example, a contentious battle has been raging in Brooklyn over a development known as Atlantic Yards, which protesters say is a sweetheart deal for developer Forest City. The trick for economic developers is to strike the proper balance between preserving community character and creating opportunity for business.

Economic developers can also be tasked with revitalizing parts of town that are underperforming. Many cities oversee community redevelopment agencies, which are tasked with identifying opportunities for ecomomic growth within the city. This often involves identifying and luring attractive businesses to different parts of town, seed-funding local small business efforts, and prioritizing areas within the city that need the most economic help. This work can range from the construction of low-income housing to the development of commercial sites to the provision of public amenities.

Developing the local economy isn't just about bringing in a big cash cow. Many communities have relied on big-ticket tenants like auto dealerships and big box retailers to boost local tax revenues. But what's gained in revenue is often lost in quality of life. Increasingly, economic development specialists are spearheading efforts to rebuild economies by providing civic projects like open spaces and plazas to create a physical sense of community in which local businesses can thrive. But the proper balance between community and opportunity has to be negotiated, and it's not always easy.

Sometimes the greatest challenge is explaining what you do. "We spend a great deal of time on communication," says Kathy Dodson (see profile next page), "because the general lay person does not understand what economic development is. That's a fairly technical term. So, we have to explain that what we're trying to do is create jobs and improve the tax base. So we have a variety of publications that go out to different markets."

Working in the field of economic development can be challenging and rewarding. It's difficult to make money out of thin air, and that's often what economic developers are tasked with doing. Sometimes it just doesn't work. But when it does, it's a crucial piece in making communities thrive and creating opportunities for people to make a good living.

Kathy Dodson

Director of Economic Development, City of El Paso, Texas

Planetizen: Tell us about your career path.

KD: My first full-time job actually was working in Mexico for an American manufacturer. My title was material analyst, but I was really responsible for supply chain issues – bringing in products, making sure the end products got out the door in time. I knew I didn't want to stay in the manufacturing industry forever, and really just wanted to learn more about tourism development in particular.

So I went to Clemson. I ended up studying there and included a lot of environmental and planning work in my studies, and ended up doing my dissertation research down in Belize in Central America looking at the economic, environmental and socio-cultural impacts of tourism development in that area.

After that, I ended up coming to El Paso, Texas and taking a job for the Chamber of Commerce here. It started out as an international business job and then I got moved into the economic development department. That was my first pure economic development job.

I then was hired away by a real estate developer, but I really knew that I liked the community building aspect of working for a nonprofit. I took a position running the Chamber of Commerce in Santa Monica, California for a little over five years, and I eventually came back to El Paso as the Director of Economic Development.

Planetizen: Can you explain for us what an economic developer does?

In El Paso we have a very specific definition.

We're responsible for creating jobs and revitalizing underperforming areas of the community. The majority of our department's efforts are spent on business expansion and retention.

We also have an entrepreneur program so that we grow our own. I think most business developers know that the majority of your jobs are going to come from your local businesses expanding.

Then we work with several partners in the community to help with small business assistance. Being able to bring more economic vitality to the parts of the community that aren't performing well is really important to us, so we spend a lot of effort on that. Right now we have a lot of soldiers coming in, so we're trying to incentivize multi-family developers, apartment builders. It's a terrible national credit market for something like that. So, how can we, in our little community, make the math work?

Fortunately, for the first time in over 30 years our unemployment rate is below the national average. But, it's still very high and we still have a poor population. So, understanding those big picture issues and understanding what your role is in trying to solve them is also really important.

The thing I love about my job is that I come to work every day to help build a better community. So, it's a huge job. We're tasked with creating jobs and revitalizing the city. So, that's exciting and challenging. But, it's certainly a reason to get up and go into work every day.

Some Significant Employers *(in alphabetical order)*

Albuquerque Economic Development Department, www.cabq.gov/econdev

Bloomington Economic Development Corporation, www.comparebloomington.org

City of Sacramento Economic Development Department, www.cityofsacramento.org/econdev

City of San Diego Economic Development Department, www.sandiego.gov/economic-development

City of San Antonio Economic Development Department, www.sanantonio.gov/edd

The Economic Development Corporation of Kansas City, www.edckc.com

Indiana Economic Development Corporation, www.in.gov/iedc

Iowa Department of Economic Development, www.iowalifechanging.com

Louisiana Economic Development, www.louisianaeconomicdevelopment.com

Michigan City Economic Development Corporation, www.mc-edc.com

Missouri Department of Economic Development, www.ded.mo.gov

The Nebraska Department of Economic Development, www.neded.org

New Mexico Economic Development Department, www.edd.state.nm.us

New York City Economic Development Corporation, www.nycedc.com

Oregon Business Development Department, www.oregon.gov/OBDD

Saratoga Economic Development Corporation, www.saratogaedc.com

Valley Economic Development Center (San Fernando Valley, CA), www.vedc.org

Sample Job Description

Job Title: Economic Development Manager
Job Type: Development
Date Posted: 05/20/2008
Organization: City of Montebello, CA
URL: www.cityofmontebello.com

Under administrative direction, to direct, manage, supervise, and coordinate the programs and activities of the Economic Development Division within the Community Development Department; responsible for the management and supervision of the professional, technical, and clerical staff of the Economic Development Division. Excellent public relations skills are essential for the Economic Development Manager position.

This position requires a B.A. in urban planning, real estate development, business, public administration, or related field. Five years of progressively responsible economic development and/or redevelopment experience for a municipal agency in California. Varied and well-rounded experience in economic development, community development, redevelopment, and housing is preferable. Also, a familiarity or experience with mixed-use, work-live, urban/downtown housing, and transit-oriented development is preferable.

Two years of experience in a supervisory, managerial, or administrative position working for a municipal agency is required. A Master's degree in a related field may substitute for one year of the supervisory experience.

More Resources

- International Economic Development Council, www.iedconline.org
- Economic Development Association (U.S. Dept. of Commerce), www.eda.gov
- Small Business Advancement National Center, www.sbaer.uca.edu

Transportation

Courtesy of Sound Transit

The Tacoma Link light rail in Tacoma, Washington opened in 2003, part of a recent boom in transit.

Transportation and mobility are some of the most visibly important aspects of any urban place. How people move from place to place often determines the flavor and feel of a city – like the wide freeways of Houston, the crowded subways of New York City, or even the aerial tram in Portland, Oregon.

And it is often the planning and location of transportation infrastructure that guides the growth of communities and regions. Transportation planners, therefore, play a powerful role in urban planning and development.

The field encompasses a wide range of responsibilities and areas of expertise. Two of those areas, transportation planner and airport planner, are profiled in this section. But you may be interested specifically in planning public transit, or even maritime planning. Specialized training and field-specific tools will be needed to do each type of work. And though deciding which track of the transportation world you want to enter doesn't have to happen right away, it is worth noting that each is distinct and carries its own set of challenges.

Transportation is also heavily influenced by the engineering field, so a working knowledge of the technical side and a love of statistics is useful.

The world is not going to stop moving, and with increasing globalization, the future of cities and their economies will likely depend on transportation planning. And with a growing popularity for light rail and commuter systems, it's a great time to consider becoming a transportation planner.

Transportation Planner

For the typical person, transportation infrastructure is probably the best understood aspect of urban planning. They interact with it daily, it helps them get to where they need to go, and when it doesn't work, they get very upset. In that regard, the transportation planner plays a major role in determining the function and mobility of the city. Because transportation is so crucial to the operation of the modern environment, transportation planning can be a very demanding job.

In the past, the transportation planner was mainly tasked with siting roads and other transportation infrastructure, working on short- and long-range transportation plans, and generally making it as easy as possible for cars and trucks to get around. Now, however, more planners and officials are beginning to look at streets as places, adding new dimensions to the realm of transportation planning. Bicycle infrastructure, transit-oriented development, issues of walkability and public health are all encompassed in the broad world of transportation planning.

Public transportation is another major component of the field, and one that many expect to balloon in the coming decades. Rising fuel prices and emerging concerns about greenhouse gas emissions have elevated public transit from a service for the poor to an environmental movement. Whether it is a new city bus line or a regional high speed rail operation, communities across the country are seeing public transportation as a critical part of their futures and their ability to compete in the global market.

But it's not all bullet trains and super-highways. Transportation planners also delve into the fine details of the mobile worlds – from parking space requirements to crosswalks to speed bumps. In addition, transportation planning is a very data-driven exercise. Transportation planners will often research mobility patterns and survey-derived data to help determine where new facilities should be planned and how to better utilize the existing infrastructure.

Transportation planners work at various levels of government from local to regional to state to federal. Metropolitan planning organizations are federally required to work with the various levels of government to plan and maintain transportation infrastructure, so there is a lot of work in these organizations.

There is also an increasingly vibrant private consulting sector engaged in transportation planning. Due to the expanding range of work associated with transportation and mobility, consultancies fill almost every niche. Whether you're interested in using smart technology to monitor highway occupancy or building dedicated bike lanes, a wide variety of firms focus on the whole gamut of projects.

A good transportation planner can think broadly about the whole system of transportation – from the most minute details to the interrelated workings of vast regional systems. That may mean monitoring transit ridership figures or laying out a new bike lane. The realm of transportation is immense, and having a comprehensive understanding is crucial. A basis in urban planning will be useful, but transportation planners are often trained as engineers. Because these two fields intertwine in the realm of transportation, a knowledge of both can be helpful. More important is a willingness to constantly learn about how a wide variety of systems and professions coalesce to create efficient and sustainable transportation systems.

Ian Sacs

Director of Transportation and Parking, City of Hoboken, NJ

Planetizen: How did you get interested in doing transportation planning, and how did you get to where you are now?

IS: From the beginning when I started my education, I always wanted to be involved in improving the environment. I actually picked environmental engineering because of the name. I really had no idea what the program entailed. It was funny when I started to realize how intense the mathematics were going to be. There were a couple of times where I thought I might back out, but the professors encouraged me to stay. Once I got out of the theory classes and into the practical applications, I realized that this is where I want to be.

As an undergrad, I was interested in water treatment systems, but when I got into grad school, I switched over to transportation. For me, it was one and the same, I knew I could work in the transportation field and still make a beneficial contribution to the environment.

But I actually find now that I'm much happier in transportation than if I had stayed in water systems, just because these are such exciting times to be involved in the transportation/planning industry. There's so much happening. There's so much change going on in the United States. To be in the middle of it and to be fortunate enough to be near such a big city and working in a big city where so much of the change is happening, it's just really thrilling.

Planetizen: What do you like best about being a transportation planner?

IS: It may sound strange, but what I like best is working with the public. Obviously, there's a lot of friction that can be generated by making changes to the way that things work. But as an engineer, I think that I'm basically interested in solving problems and finding the right solution and the best solution. Understanding the problem and talking through what the right solution is, and getting to the point where the community is happy and seeing that physically change in the community and watching the results of that, that's what I like the best.

Planetizen: What is the most challenging aspect of your job?

IS: I think it's trying to find the right balance between being passionate about one's profession and also realizing that you've got to pay attention to your personal life as well.

It's so easy, particularly in consulting, I think, to find yourself working 70- or 80-hour weeks and just be completely immersed in the work all day long and then heading out in the evenings to attend council meetings or testifying at zoning boards. One could do that for many, many years and then realize that they've missed out on stuff. It's definitely a struggle and it's a big challenge to make sure that one can find some reprieve and some escape and relax the brain a little bit.

The more exposure you have to the industry and the more involvement you have on projects, the more people want you to be involved, assuming you've got some skill at it, and so you can fast-track your career by pumping as much of your time into the work as possible. So there definitely is a challenge in striking that balance, and each individual has to choose what that's going to be for them.

Planetizen: What would you offer as advice to someone who is interested in entering the field as a transportation planner?

IS: I think the most important advice, from my perspective, is to really understand all of the issues as best as possible, particularly what the community concerns are, before jumping to conclusions on what the right answer is. I think all of us coming out of school are really excited because we're learning the state of the practice. We're learning the most progressive ideas, and we're anxious to jump out into the real world and do good things.

Perhaps the biggest fault of planners when we're young is to immediately think that we know what the answer is and not listen enough to the community's concerns and to really pick the right solution. Oftentimes, it's never as clear-cut as what's explained in the textbooks, there's always some mesh or blend that's required to make things work, and it takes a long time to kind of get the gut reaction to come up with the right solution very quickly. So, when we're younger it's most important to spend the time and really think about all the different issues involved before jumping to an answer.

Some Significant Employers *(in alphabetical order)*

AECOM, www.aecom.com/What+We+Do/Transportation

City of Los Angeles Department of Transportation, www.ladot.lacity.org

New York City Department of Transportation, www.nyc.gov/html/dot/html/about/employ.shtml

Texas Transportation Institute, http://tti.tamu.edu

U.S. Department of Transportation, www.dot.gov

Sample Job Description

Job Title: Transportation Planner/ Senior Transportation Planner
Job Type: Transportation
Date Posted: 06/13/2009
Organization: Ada County Highway District
URL: www.achd.ada.id.us

Applications are now being accepted for the position of Transportation Planner/ Sr. Transportation Planner in the Planning & Programming Department. Starting Wage is DOQ, plus excellent benefits! (May come in at a Sr. Transportation Planner level if qualifications / experience are appropriate.)

Primary Responsibilities:
- Conducts the District's planning and programming efforts, including outreach to area agencies and the general public and other job-related duties as required.
- Responsible for the District's medium and long range transportation plans, integration of transportation and land use planning, and coordination with area agencies on other planning initiatives including Comprehensive Plans and transit planning.
- Serves as a technical resource to District employees and other agencies/organizations involved in the various transportation programs.

Qualifications:
- Must have proven ability to facilitate constructive dialogue related to complex policy and planning issues. Must have knowledge of: Federal and State regulations as related to transportation planning specific job tasks; Planning methodologies, specifically long and short range transportation planning; Federal, state and local government structures and federal aid programming; Roadway projects, including technical aspects, planning, budgeting, construction and scheduling; Engineering principles and practices; Technical writing methods; ACHD Policy Manual; and Land use planning.
- Proficiency in Word, Excel, and Access is a must. Knowledge of OnPoint, Visio and Microsoft Projects is a plus.
- A Bachelor's degree in Transportation Planning, Urban Planning, Public Administration, Engineering or a related field is preferred. Previous experience is a plus. Sr. Transportation Planner level must have three yrs of relevant experience and AICP is preferred.
  OR
- An equivalent combination of experience and training that provides the required knowledge, skills and abilities may be acceptable.

More Resources

- American Planning Association, Transportation Planning Division, www.apa-tpd.org
- American Public Transportation Association, www.apta.com
- National Center for Bicycling and Walking, www.bikefed.org
- Transportation Research Board, http://nationalacademies.org/trb
- American Association of State Highway and Transportation Officials, www.transportation.org

Airport Planner

Airport, or aviation, planning is one of the more unusual niches in public planning. Like other forms of transportation planning such as maritime and military planning, airport planners primarily engage in long-term land use planning and working with local communities.

Airport planning can be challenging, because airports are seen by many as a noxious land use. Ryan N. Hall is an airport planner with the San Diego County Regional Airport Authority, and he regularly runs into issues with this bad reputation. "The sad fact is that airports have a perception of being undesirable," says Hall. "They are loud, create traffic, emit air pollution, bring in-laws that you never want to see, and are generally a hassle to deal with on any given day."

This means fewer airports are being built, even as demand grows. "With no new airports coming online anytime soon, we are being forced into handling record passenger loads with the airports that were mostly designed and built in the 1930s and 1940s," says Hall. This is going to be a challenge for growing commmunities, but maybe even more so for the people who have to make the case that these "undesirable" land uses actually are necessary.

In this light, airport planners need to be adept at consensus building. In order to get any expansion built, airport planners often have to work with all of the local stakeholders for years, including everyone from homeowners to local governments to utilities.

But once plans are approved and expansions move ahead, there's still work to be done. Because it can take a very long time to see results, airport planners like Dan Wong (profiled in this section) sometimes work in an operational capacity rather than focusing strictly on land use.

Planning the land use of an airport involves creating strategies to enhance capacity, balance terminal functions and improve airport performance. Planners do this by addressing key design issues and transportation flow – from people at security gates to baggage trucks on the tarmac.

Because of the wide variety of transportation modes in play at any given time, airports are often on the cutting edge of transportation technologies. They've implemented monorails, personal rapid transit, and other sorts of innovative peoplemovers long before cities have. In large part, planners are able to experiment with projects and technologies like these because the community they serve is only around for a few hours. They don't have a protesting public or angry homeowners within the airport opposing or interfering in their decisions on airport grounds. Within the bounds of the airport, it's like a personal playset for planning.

It is likely that the need for airport planning is only going to increase in the coming years. The economy is only becoming more global, and telecommuting can't replace face-to-face networking. As airports and nations try to keep up with the rising demand, it will be airport planners who guide the future of travel infrastructure – and who are tasked with meeting the travel needs of a globalizing world.

Dan Wong

Airport Planner, City and County of San Francisco

Planetizen: Can you tell us about your career path?

DW: I had just walked away from law school back in 1983, and I decided I've always wanted to do something in transportation. My parents basically said if I wanted to finish law school they'd pay for it, but if I wanted to do something in transportation I'd have to pay for it myself. I looked at transportation engineering which would have taken me four years to complete, and since transportation planning would take me only two years, and I only had enough money for two years, I chose the planning route. I ended up at San Jose State, because it was one of the few schools that allowed me to have an internship and attend school because it's a late afternoon/evening program. At that time, at SJ State, I was one of the only transportation planning students there. Everyone wanted to go into land use, I was the oddball at that time.

I got an internship at Muni, the municipal railway of San Francisco, in the planning department. It was a great position to be in, because I could interview city employees for my master's paper. I had access to people you would otherwise never get access to. My graduation present from Muni was "Congratulations, you're a planner."

I ended up here at the airport because the airport has its own transit system, and they needed somebody. It was a promotion to become a full planner at the airport. Muni wasn't hiring full planners at the time – I would have been stuck there indefinitely as an associate.

My initial job was to run the airport's

surface transportation. I got to work on all sorts of projects including the transportation element for the new international terminal at the airport.

My role is service planning, or what they call operations planning. We make decisions short term, quick, we're day-to-day stuff and within the next three to four months. One of our assignments from the last couple of weeks was to design a bus system that will run between the airport terminal building and the Millbrae BART station. Our staff here had several days to put that together, and it was implemented on July 1st, 2009. That's what we do.

Planetizen: What are the rewards and challenges of being an airport planner?

DW: The part I love the best about my career choice and what I have become is I can make decisions that can be implemented immediately. It's a separate arena from the rest of mainstream planning but it's still useful and it takes all of my planning skills.

As far as challenges go, planning has not always been looked on as a necessary element of airport staff. Most people who are in airports come from aviation. They may be former military. Here in San Francisco, the staff is very accepting of planning, but in other airports you sometimes have to convince the traditional airport types that planning is a necessary, worthwhile function into which airports should invest time and money.

Planetizen: What attributes make someone well suited to be an airport planner?

DW: The ability to work with people. In an airport you have to work with a lot of different clientele — ground transportation providers, other public agencies like SamTrans, CalTrain, and BART. You have to have great communication skills, both oral and written. You have to be able to convey what you know and what you want people to do, in a way that's not threatening yet gets the point across. You have to be able to convey that immediately — otherwise you're going to get walked all over.

Some Significant Employers *(in alphabetical order)*

Airport and Aviation Professionals, Inc., www.avairpros.com

Airport Planning and Development Ltd (APD), www.apd-airports.com

The Benham Companies, LLC, www.benham.com

Boyd Group International, www.aviationplanning.com

Federal Aviation Administration, Office of Airport Planning and Programming, www.faa.gov

Halcrow, www.halcrow.com

Mead & Hunt, www.meadhunt.com

The PBSJ Corporation, www.pbsj.com

PennDOT's Bureau of Aviation Planning, www.dot.state.pa.us

RS&H, www.rsandh.com

Transport and Logistics Consultancy, www.tlconsult.com

URS Corporation, www.urs.apply2jobs.com

Washington State Department of Transportation, www.wsdot.wa.gov

Sample Job Description

Job Title: Experienced Airport Planner
Job Type: Planner
Date Posted: 09/08/2008
Organization: Mead & Hunt, Inc.
URL: www.meadhunt.com

Mead & Hunt's aviation practice is growing and there are exceptional opportunities for experienced airport planners to join and grow with the firm. Mead & Hunt is the 17th largest aviation consulting firm in the U.S. and has been rated one of the top ten consulting firms for which to work. Responsibilities of our airport planners include but are not limited to: writing aviation, environmental, and land use planning documents, researching aviation related issues; developing activity forecasts; and general project management. Travel will be necessary.

The successful candidate must have a bachelor's degree or higher in urban planning, aviation management, or civil engineering and at least three years of experience in the airport planning consulting field.

The ideal candidate will have any/ all of the following: AICP registration or a PE license; excellent research and writing skills; strong communication skills; GIS and/or CAD experience; project management experience; ability to meet deadlines; ability to take initiative and be a self-starter; ability to work well independently; a team-player attitude; excellent interpersonal skills; strong organizational skills.

MEAD & HUNT, Inc.
Attn: HR
6501 Watts Road
Madison, WI 53719

www.meadhunt.com
Affirmative Action / Equal Opportunity Employer
hr@meadhunt.com

More Resources

- *Airport Planning & Management*, by Alexander T. Wells and Seth Young, 2004, McGraw-Hill
- Federal Aviation Administration, Office of Airport Planning and Programming, www.faa.gov/about/office_org/headquarters_offices/arp/offices/app
- International Air Transport Association, www.iata.org/training/courses/tapp08

Politics

Cong. Earl Blumenauer of Oregon, a vocal advocate for expanding transportation options.

Courtesy of the office of Earl Blumenauer

While urban planning is a highly regulated field, with codes, zoning and processes in place to ensure that no preferential treatment is given, politics retains a hold over the process. Planning commissions are politically appointed, and they have the last word over recommendations of planning staff. City councils and mayors make decisions over where funding goes and what neighborhoods get the most attention. If you're looking to make a difference in affordable housing, transportation and neighbohood renewal, the political fray could be the right venue for you.

The other way to influence the political agenda is to work at an advocacy organization. Most people are more familiar with groups like The National Rifle Association and PETA, but there are a great number of nonprofit organizations working to influence urban issues like transportation policy, equity in housing, and historic preservation. Groups like the American Public Transportation Association (APTA) and Transportation for America have significant influence over how transit dollars get spent in the United States. Even groups like AARP have divisions that advocate on behalf of their consistuents to influence policy on land use issues.

There is a debate in the field of urban planning around whether planners can take an advocacy role, or if their job is merely to be a conduit between the community and the politicians who make the decisions. If planning's lack of direct decisionmaking would be difficult for you, you may consider steering into a career in the political realm.

Public Policy

Are you a rabble-rouser? Do you get satisfaction from persuading people to be passionate about a cause? Then public policy might be the career for you. There are thousands of organizations around the country fighting for local, regional and national issues around land use, and their power is growing.

There is not a lot of consensus over job titles in the public policy world, and that tends to be the case because advocacy groups often grow organically and people end up wearing a lot of hats. Titles range from Project Coordinator to Public Policy Expert to Campaign Manager. Much of the work involves getting people or groups to come together and agree on a policy, then take collective action to influence the government on that policy.

But well-crafted policy platforms don't come out of thin air: the other side of effective advocacy is solid research, or at least, finding ways to translate solid research into something the public understands. The pairing of irrefutable data with great communications techniques is hard to beat.

"It makes my job easier," says Jacqueline Grimshaw (profiled next page), "if I'm able to say that this research has been done, either by us or by somebody else, and to see the light-bulb go off in the legislator's face when you've actually made the sale, so to speak, and they get it. It's terrific."

While national organizations get the spotlight, there are numerous groups advocating on the local level that manage to have a lot of influence on the conversation. The Michigan Land Use Institute, for example, has worked since 1995 to "to help Michigan avoid the patterns of suburban sprawl and over-development that cause traffic congestion, pollution, loss of community, rising costs to individuals and governments, and a deteriorating quality of life." Groups like MLUI exist in most major areas of the country, and have been ahead of the curve in thinking about urban planning issues as a regional problem. Their expertise and persistence in publicizing specific issues often plays a major role in the creation of policies and legislation.

And indeed it is the sheer amount of these groups that gives them such power — not because they operate as one large unit, but because each has its own niche into which it focuses specifically and intensely. These niche issues range from low-income housing solutions to senior citizen mobility to street calming. By centering their work around these issues, advocacy groups are able to share a depth of knowledge with the public and the elected officials who serve them.

Jobs in public policy goups are often labors of love. People will get involved with groups they feel passionate about. Sometimes that means working for little or even no money. But any person with enough drive and interest in a specific topic should be able to turn a low-paying or no-paying gig into a viable profession. Whether it's a small group working to improve bicycle safety in one city or a nationally-focused organization lobbying Congress for expanded high speed rail funding, those most invested in the ideals behind the movement are those most likely to be successful within the field.

Making public policy is no easy task, and navigating the realm of politics takes patience, skill and elbow grease. But the payoffs for pushing through a new project or policy proposal will make the hard work seem like nothing at all. And for those interested in urban planning, crafting and implementing policies that help people and improve cities is the ultimate reward.

Jaquelyne Grimshaw

Vice President for Policy, The Center for Neighborhood Technology.

Planetizen: What was your first job out of school?

JG: My career path was totally serendipitous. I was out of school, and I was going downtown on Lakeshore Drive in Chicago. Someone ran into the back of me after I stopped to avoid hitting a car that was in the travel lane. I ended up being taken to Michael Reese hospital as an emergency patient. I was just out of school, so the only physician I had was my pediatrician. So my mother's physician ended up treating me. As I was getting better from my injuries, he asked me about my career. I said, "I don't know. I just graduated, and I really don't know what I am going to do." He said, "Well, why don't you work here at the hospital." He sent me to personnel, and they were actually looking for research lab techs in hematology.

So, that was my first job out of college. Every step after that has been the same kind of by-chance encounter that has led me from one career to another. I have never gone out and actually applied for a job in my whole career.

I went from working for children and family services to being asked to take over this program for the state of Illinois. It was a model employer program designed to recruit women, minorities, and veterans into state government. Then in politics, the governor that I was working for lost the election and another governor came in. I ended up being switched from personnel over to labor with this work incentive program, which was helping folks on welfare to get jobs.

So I went and I did that for the state. The guy I was working for the state was actually a fed that was on loan to the state. He went back to the feds and asked me to come over to the feds with them. And so then I ended up working for the federal government still doing the work incentive program.

Harold Washington was a longtime friend of mine. He ran for mayor of Chicago and won, and he asked me to come and work for the mayor's office. So I ended up working for the mayor's office in intergovernmental affairs. The job of intergovernmental affairs is to be the liaison between the mayor's office and all of these governments that were coterminous with the city of Chicago. And that included our finance planning agency, our transportation planning agency, our storm order agency. Illinois is blessed with a gazillion units of government and they have overlapping borders, so my job was to articulate the mayor's policy to all of these different agencies. And so that got me started on land use and transportation and dealing with these agencies.

Planetizen: So having worked in a lot of government positions, what do you see as the difference between that and working for a nonprofit, public policy group?

JG: One, we get to define the agenda. When you're working for government somebody else is doing that. Somebody else was making those decisions and the only thing I could do was to implement decisions someone else had made. At the nonprofit level we get to decide what rules we want to change, what policies we want to implement, he strategy for going about doing that, the timing for when we do that, the funding to support doing that. I mean, it's all determined by us. The only things that are out of our control are the calendars. If we're talking about legislation, every legislature has their own calendar and they set that, and of course we have to exist within that calendar, but in terms of the content or the project or the outcomes, we are totally responsible which is, to me, a much better way of being.

Planetizen: What do you like best about doing the kind of work that you do, and what do you find the most challenging?

JG: Doing the work that I do I really get to see the results. It is gratifying to have an idea, to figure out how to implement that idea, to develop or create or access the resources in order to make this idea work, and then to work out the pros, the cons, the barriers, the whatever, that need to be overcome to make it happen, and then seeing it happen. It's like fireworks going off when you get to the end stage and you've actually changed the world a little bit.

Some Significant Public Policy Groups *(in alphabetical order)*

American Assocation of State and Highway Officials (AASHTO), www.transportation.org

Center for an Urban Future, www.nycfuture.org

Michigan Land Use Institute, http://mlui.org

Reconnecting America, www.reconnectingamerica.org

Sierra Club, www.sierraclub.org

TransForm, http://transformca.org

Transportation for America, http://t4america.org

Sample Job Description

Job Title: Project Coordinator
Job Type: Politics
Date Posted: 07/11/2009
Organization: Rogue Advocates
URL: www.rogueadvocates.org

We are currently looking for a Project Coordinator for Rogue Advocates, a 503(c)(3) non-profit organization focusing on land use advocacy in the beautiful Rogue Valley of Southern Oregon.

Rogue Advocates' core geographical interests are private lands in Jackson and Josephine counties, but our land use concerns are the Rogue Valley basin-wide.

Our objectives in land use are twofold:
1) Advocacy: We track and provide basic information on land use decisions in Josephine and Jackson counties to assist in providing awareness of land use activities occurring in the Rogue Valley. We work to assure that regional land use decisions comply with all current land use laws and regulations and are compatible with a common sense vision for a sustainable and livable Rogue Valley by actively participating in the land use process for certain projects we feel warrant our attention. We also review and comment on proposed legislation; and; 2) Outreach: We work to provide education on the threats to the long-term livability of the Rogue Valley. Working through regional media outlets and networking with community groups, we keep land use activities in the forefront of public awareness.

We are looking for a diverse, motivated, determined, and organized individual that can assist Rogue Advocates in becoming a prominent Land Use Advocate in the Rogue Valley.

Ideal candidates will have knowledge of the statewide planning program in Oregon. However, we are open to accepting applications from individuals who are competent to perform the other mentioned duties and have a willingness to delve into the legalistic world of land use planning in Oregon. Ideal candidates will have a J.D. or Master's Degree in a land use or related field.

More Resources

- Idealist, www.idealist.org
- *Advocacy and Pluralism in Planning,* an influential article by Paul Davidoff
- Lincoln Institute of Land Policy, www.lincolninst.edu
- Land Use Policy Journal, www.elsevier.com
- Journal of the American Planning Association, www.planning.org/japa

Commissioner

The role of planning commissioner is not exactly a "job." You don't apply, you don't go in every day, and — maybe most importantly — you don't get paid. It's an appointed position to a board that serves the governing body of the local town, city or municipality, advising specifically on land use decisions. Planning commissions are, for the most part, advisory bodies, but they can wield a fair amount of power in local land use and development decisions. Much of that power, though, depends on the quality, knowledge and experience of the members of the commission.

Planning commissioners don't necessarily need planning-related education or experience, but both help. What may be even more valuable is a desire to improve and serve the community. Because local officials often rely on the judgment of planning commissions as they vote on development projects they may have been too busy to deeply investigate, the more commissioners care about the future of their communities, the better they can guide the officials empowered to bring about community change.

Planning commissions typically meet once a month to discuss local land use proposals and issues. Commissioners are usually tasked with reviewing project documentation and general plans, performing site visits, and crafting policy recommendations. And though a position on a planning commission is explicitly not a job, the most effective commissioners often treat it as if it were.

Broad knowledge about planning issues, rules and innovations helps a commissioner play a useful role on what is essentially a panel of experts. The more knowledgeable a planning commissioner is, the better able the commission is to guide officials towards making good decisions for the community.

Many planning commissioners are considered "citizen planners" — people who don't have any previous planning knowledge per se but who have a deep interest in the subject. But it is also common to see people with many years of planning knowledge and experience, from PhDs in urban planning to decades on city planning staffs.

As a longtime planning commissioner and columnist for the quarterly publication Planning Commissioners Journal, Ric Stephens (profiled on the next page) has been offering advice to planning commissioners for years. He suggests that planners at any level should consider taking on the role of planning commissioner at some point, as the service provides an outside perspective on the role of planning departments. By serving as a middleman between the public and city officials, planning commissioners can gain a more holistic view of the process of planning.

Serving on a planning commission may not be the first step right out of college, but Stephens says planners should consider the prospect of serving as a commissioner at some point. Because the planning commissioner can simultaneously play the role of interested citizen, advocate and activist, the service offers a well-rounded experience in the planning process. By understanding those various roles, planners who serve as a planning commissioners will be better equipped to respond to the variety of concerns and perspectives held by those involved in community planning at all levels. This comprehensive understanding will better enable them to empathize with and respond to what are typically strong opinions on these local land use issues. A commissioner who is patient, a good listener and a calm communicator would be a valuable asset to any community.

Ric Stephens

Planning Commissioner, City of Beaverton, OR

Planetizen: Explain your career path and how you got to where you are now.

RS: My interest early on was psychology – but mainly as it relates to geography and community. So, I had an undergraduate degree in psychology studying environment and perception and then got employed with an engineering firm doing planning work and went back to school to study more about the planning side of that. It was an unusual way to get involved in planning.

I have been a commissioner for the City of Hemet, California, the City of Riverside, California, and now the City of Beaverton. I was also an airport lands commissioner for Riverside County for five years. My civic service side goes back quite a long ways. I've been a planning commissioner for, I think, collectively more than 15 years now.

Planetizen: Describe a typical day in your role as a planning commissioner.

RS: I would hate for people to think that being a planning commissioner takes a full day. It's a small amount of time. For most commissioners it is a volunteer item. So, the tasks that I would be doing as the planning commissioner would be to read the staff report, visit the site, and then attend the actual hearing.

Our hearings are in the evening from 6:30 and usually over by 10:00 or 11:00, sometimes 1:00 in the morning, but usually they are finished by 10:00. That basically completes the whole spectrum of activities. It may be, in an entire month, eight to 16 hours total at the most.

Planetizen: What you like best about serving as a planning commissioner?

RS: There are, I think, four compelling reasons to do it. One is the civic service side. It's just doing something for the community where I live. I think that's a really important one. The second one is advocacy. There are some issues that I feel very strongly about. I wanted to be a planning commissioner so that I can help promote those issues. I think the third one is being engaged with the community. To me, that's really important being a fairly new resident up here. And the last one, the one that I think is the most compelling to me personally, is it's a very good learning experience. When I go to the hearings and read the cases, I learn so much about people and place making. It's like going to school all the time. It's really a unique opportunity and so open to planners. There are so few planners who take the time or interest to get involved in commissions and boards.

Planetizen: If you were to talk to someone considering taking on a role as planning commissioner, what advice would you offer them?

RS: First of all, to understand why they want to be a planning commissioner, and then understanding that to be successful and to be happy as a planning commissioner they will have to understand how they can balance the needs of the community with achieving those objectives that they have about being a commissioner.

I hope that doesn't sound too obtuse, but, for example, if the real reason they want to be a planning commissioner is to be an advocate for something, and their cause is something that goes against the grain of the community, then they'll be unhappy and probably very unsuccessful.

Planetizen: If you were to start your career over today, what, if anything, would you do differently?

RS: There's so many things. I think I would start out feeling more capable about doing things. I've been doing work in more than 25 countries overseas. People always ask, "Well, how did you get to do that?" I have to say the answer is really simple. There are tons of opportunities to work overseas.

The sad thing is I think people limit themselves, planners limit themselves by not thinking that they're either capable or that there are opportunities. I could have been doing international work and a variety of other things that I am doing today much, much earlier in my career if I had been more confident about doing those things.

Some Significant Planning Commissions *(in alphabetical order)*

City of Jacksonville Planning Commission
www.coj.net/Departments/Regulatory+Boards+and+Commissions/Planning+Commission

Dallas City Plan Commission, www.dallascityhall.com/development_services/plan_commission.html

Denver Planning Board, www.denvergov.org/planning/PlanningBoard/tabid/431851

Los Angeles City Planning Commission, http://cityplanning.lacity.org

New York City Planning Commission, www.nyc.gov/html/dcp/html/about/plancom.shtml

Philadelphia City Planning Commission, www.philaplanning.org

Phoenix Planning Commission, www.phoenix.gov/PLANNING

St. Louis County Planning Commission, www.co.st-louis.mo.us/plan/zone.html

Sample Job Description

Job Title: Planning Commissioner
Job Type: Politics
Date Posted: 07/31/2009
Organization: City of Edgewood, WA, Planning Commission
URL: www.cityofedgewood.org

The basic responsibilities of the commission include:

- Provide recommendations to the City Council for development and review of the comprehensive plan.
- Provide recommendations to the City Council on the zoning map and table of permitted uses.
- Provide recommendations to the City Council on amendments to the development regulations.

Specific tasks include, but are not limited to:
- Review and comment on the proposed multi-year comprehensive plan work program and budget, proposed citizen participation plan for the preparation of the comprehensive plan, and proposed planning area boundary.
- Review and make recommendations on the proposed level of service standards and the preparation of each of the elements of the comprehensive plan.
- Review all elements of the comprehensive plan for consistency.
- Review and recommend changes to the City's development regulations, zoning map and table of permitted uses consistent with the comprehensive plan.
- Review and make recommendations on any proposed impact fees that the City may be considering.
- Conduct research and make recommendations on issues of interest to the City Council.

The City Council shall seek to ensure representation includes members with an understanding of architecture and urban planning, economic development, community involvement, and knowledge of the specific concerns of Edgewood residents. Furthermore, the Council shall seek a diverse membership that includes residents from each geographic region of the City, owners or operators of Edgewood businesses, and citizens with a record of community involvement. Each member of the commission must be a City resident. The work of the Planning Commission will be conducted in a small group environment and members will be required to work effectively with a team of diverse members.

More Resources
- American Planning Association Publications, "The Commissioner" www.planning.org/thecommissioner
- Planetizen's Planning Commissioner Training Course www.planetizen.com/courses/plan315
- Planning Commissioners Journal, www.plannersweb.com
- Preservation Directory, www.preservationdirectory.com
- The Planning Commissioner's Book, http://ceres.ca.gov/planning/plan_comm

Politician

Planners and politicians sit on different sides of the podium. One group develops ideas, the other approves them (or not). One is hired, the other is elected. One writes policy, the other defends it. And though they are so different, planners and politicians rely heavily on one another and come to understand each other's role very well. That's why it's not too far of a stretch to cross the border and go from planner to politician.

"Many of the more politically astute planners eventually change careers and become community development directors, city managers or county administrators." says Richard H. Carson, who worked for years as a city planning director. "It would be fair to characterize such people as 'paid politicians.' Political, strategic and organizational planning skills are as important as land use planning skills to such people."

A life in politics is about being able to motivate people to move towards a certain goal. Therefore, the life of a politician is intensely social. If you don't draw energy from engaging other people, then this isn't the career for you. Public appearances are a constant, and inspiration is the politician's tool. At the same time, you need to have a thick skin and an even demeanour even as your name is being cursed.

When it come to local land use decisions, city councilpersons and the mayor sit on top of the pyramid. The planning commission's decision is usually just a 'recommendation', and the city council has the final say. This applies to everything from okaying building projects to approving amendments to the planning code. In San Francisco, the Board of Supervisors weighs in on decisions as small as purchasing more parking meters.

So if want a say in local land use decisions, you can't do much better than being a councilperson or mayor.

Of course, it's a competitive career choice. But unlike careers such as academic or architect, rigorous academic training is not absolutely necessary. What is required is membership, in anything and everything. The more groups you are an active part in, the more constituents you can count on for their vote.

Thinking bigger? You might move your way up to state or national politics. At this level, you are beholden to your local district, certainly, but your picture expands greatly. Legislation is a powerful tool when it comes to land use. Even as local jurisdictions hold on to what buildings get built where, statewide legislation can control things like protecting coastlines from development, requiring green building practices, and controlling vehicle emissions.

Congressman Earl Blumenauer (D-OR) is a case study in how to bring land use issues to a national stage. He has used his position on the House Transportation and Infrastructure Committee to promote ideas like smart growth, transit expansion, and bicycle infrastructure. In 1991, he created a "Bike Caucus" in Washington as a way to bring attention to policies that aim to integrate bicycling as an attractive transportation option.

Whatever forum you aspire to, politics involves creating consensus and a lot of diplomacy. The ability to sympathize with all sides of an issue and show people you understand their concerns is paramount. The ability to actually create useful change once that synthesis is complete – well, that's the great challenge of politics.

Ann Cheng

City Councilperson, City of El Cerrito

Planetizen: What was your career path?

AC: The thing that launched me into the planning career and opened my eyes to that, was when I went to an environmental law conference at Davis, where a professor said, "All right kids, if you want to change the world you have to know how local government works because, at least in California, this is where all the decisions are made about where things get built, how they get built, or what doesn't get built."

I'd never had a professor say point blank, "This is how you change the world." So I thought, "I'm going to take that to heart and figure out what that means."

From there, my first permanent job out of college was working for the Contra Costa County Community Development Department. My marketable skill that helped me transition from biology to planning was GIS. With GIS I helped do watershed mapping and helped the county move from paper to digital maps.

From there, I went into redevelopment because I wanted to work with the lower-income communities of Contra Costa County. Bay Point, Rodeo, and El Sobrante. These communities had creek issues that intersected with planning for the built environment. Eventually I got a job with Alta Planning + Design, which is a non-motorized transportation planning firm focused on pedestrian and bicycle infrastructure.

Planetizen: In November of 2008, you ran for a seat on the El Cerrito, California City Council and won. What do you feel are the rewards and challenges of being a city councilperson?

AC: The hardest part has been figuring out the protocols. How do you get things on the agenda? Figuring out where I stand because I'm new to the council role, because I'm young and also an advocate.

Also figuring out how to best use my time, because there's so much information to process. We receive information packets weekly about the decisions we'll be considering, and they're regularly 1-2 inches thick. I usually have at least two official council meetings a month, and receive meeting agendas and packets 72 hours before. I usually review my council packets over the weekend and check in with my city manager to clarify information and bring up issues that come up as I review the packet.

On top of that I'm also a liaison to a couple of other committees like the economic development board or the design review board. I'm also on the San Pablo Avenue Specific Plan Advisory Committee. There are so many issues that come up. So, knowing which issues are best for me to weigh in on, given my unique perspective as an urban planner, is really important.

The rewards are meeting people who are also passionate and want to get involved and help El Cerrito realize its potential as a liveable, wonderful community. The more people bring in their good ideas, the better.

I also think it's liberating working as a councilperson because unlike the planner at the government agency, you're in the decision-making role, you're driving things, setting policy. Versus life as a staff planner or an advocate, where you're proposing ideas and you're getting shot down. Now I'm in this new position, which will take some getting used to.

The best part is getting to bring all the great ideas I come across in my work at Trans-Form, with the Great Communities Collaborative and now GreenTRIP, strait to El Cerrito staff and council for consideration. Being younger and Asian, I also think its really important that I represent a perspective that is usually missing.

Planetizen: What advice would you give someone who is interested in becoming a city councilperson?

AC: Wherever you're at in your career, if you're maybe already a planner, just try to get involved with as many things as possible. You need to make the time to step up and get in the mix. It takes more work, but then the more you do the more you get.

Some Significant City Councils (in alphabetical order)

Atlanta City Council, http://citycouncil.atlantaga.gov

Boston City Council, www.cityofboston.gov/CITYCOUNCIL

Chicago City Council, http://egov.cityofchicago.org

Dallas City Council, www.dallascityhall.com/government/government.html

Denver City Council, www.denvergov.org

Honolulu City Council, www.co.honolulu.hi.us

Houston City Council, www.houstontx.gov/council

City of Los Angeles Council, http://lacity.org/lacity/YourGovernment/CityCouncil

Miami City Commission, www.miamigov.com/City_Officials

Minneapolis City Council, www.ci.minneapolis.mn.us/council

The New York City Council, http://council.nyc.gov

Philadelphia City Council, www.phila.gov/citycouncil

Phoenix City Council, www.phoenix.gov/mayorcouncil/index.html

Sample Job Description

Job Title: Mayor
Job Type: Politics
Date Posted: Non-specific
Organization: City of Aberdeen, ND
URL: www.aberdeen.sd.us

As the Official Head of the City, the Mayor provides leadership and vision for the City of Aberdeen through the formulation of policies, delivery of city services, communication and outreach to citizens and the greater community. As head of the executive branch of government, the Mayor establishes priorities for the departments in serving the citizens of Aberdeen. The Mayor is responsible for the coordination and monitoring of policies and programs designed to meet the goals set forth by the community at large. These activities are carried out collaboratively with the City Commission.

Primary Responsibilities:
- Actively promote and implement goals set forth within the City Comprehensive Plan; revisiting the plan annually.
- Pro-actively participates and supports the community entities involved with the following: Business Retention, Business Attraction and Recruitment, Community Marketing, Tourism, Education, and Arts and Cultural Affairs.
- Solicits and receives input on community issues from constituents, staff, department heads, businesses, and those affected by policies and procedures.
- Reviews and Approves Capital Improvement expenditures based on the appropriateness to established goal the city and emerging community needs and issues.
- Serve as the City's representative and liaison in cooperative efforts with the State of SD, the South Dakota Legislature, federal agencies, surrounding counties and municipalities.

Duties of the Office:
- Performs public relations duties on behalf of the community including State of the City address and other public statements, greetings, speeches, site visits, etc.
- Defends City issues and programs
- Presides over City commission meetings and sets and interprets rules governing proceedings.
- Execute official documents such as ordinances, contracts and other documents authorized by the commission.
- Participates in special study subcommittees or task forces and coordinates necessary research., etc.

More Resources

- City Mayors, www.citymayors.com
- The United States Conference of Mayors, http://usmayors.org
- State and Local Governments (Library of Congress), www.loc.gov/rr/news/stategov/stategov.html
- Congress.org, a news and information website dedicated to civic participation www.congress.org

Research

Professors Aaron Golub (left) and Nabil Kamel of Arizona State University partner with cities on urban planning projects.

Chances are if there's a hot idea bouncing around Washington or your local government, it didn't actually come from your elected leader. Most likely it came from a think tank, research institute, or university.

There are numerous groups across the nation attempting to influence local, regional or national policy through their research, ranging from the free-market Cato Institute (home of Randal O'Toole, an outspoken critic of public transit) to the Brookings Institution (their ideas for revitalizing the Rust Belt showed up in candidate Barack Obama's platform).

Statistical analysis and hardcore data are a given in urban research. Navigating this data takes a lot of time, and often a few letters after your name. But with a wide range of groups pulling together reports and studies, there is hardly a shortage of information to be read and understood.

Identifying data sources and recent research takes a great deal of focus, and there is a broad and growing field of researchers whose main job is to make sure current trends and reports are available and usable.

And while finding and manipulating all that data is one thing, processing it and presenting it in a format people will actually understand is an entirely different but equally sophisticated task. Because the vast majority of people – policymakers included – are never going to pick up an academic journal. So, making that information approachable is a critical part of putting it into action.

Though not exactly the typical planning job, the field of research is vibrant and full of opportunity to create real change.

Academic

To some degree, the role of an urban planning academic is one that most of us understand intuitively. If you've been to college, you know what it is a professor does – prepare lectures, grade assignments, work with students.

But the assumption that professors work only six hours a week when they are teaching class is no longer the case, if it was ever true, says Ann Forsyth, professor of City and Regional Planning at Cornell University. "Today academics work year-round, raising grant funds and managing grant outcomes; providing public outreach and interacting with communities; publicizing planning to the public and their research to the profession; and they also do a lot of administration."

"They do this," says Forsyth, "largely because they either love to teach or want to contribute to knowledge, which means understanding the frontiers of particular questions. Some do both."

The old "publish or perish" cliché applies as well to urban planning academics, so if you're interested in being an academic you should have a love of writing and research. Professors are often expected to write semi-regularly for peer-reviewed journals like the *Journal of Urban Planning and Development* and the *Journal of Transport and Land Use*. Academics like Donald Shoup at UCLA and Christopher B. Leinberger at the University of Michigan regularly write books on their research and are considered thought leaders, extending their influence far beyond campus.

Lance Freeman, an assistant professor at Columbia University (profiled on the next page) chose academia for that very reason. "Working as a planner, it was difficult to really have significant effects at a policy level," says Freeman. "I thought, why don't I go into academia where I can actually write about policies." Academics may even find themselves tapped for political appointments. Xavier de Sousa Briggs, for example, went from Associate Professor of Sociology and Urban Planning at MIT to a position in the Obama administration as associate director of the White House Office of Management and Budget.

Academics also often find themselves engaged in local land use issues. To give their students a real-world perspective, many schools create courses that engage a community in a real planning process. In this way, the professor becomes the head of a team of student planners in an ersatz planning consultancy. At San José State University, for example, they've created a program called "CommUniverCity" that combines the talents of professors and students with city planning staff and neighborhood associations to work with communities in need.

Urban planning professors may also find that they are seen as experts by the media, and asked to speak to local issues. For example, Phil Ashton, assistant professor of urban planning and policy at University of Illinois at Chicago, is often quoted as an expert on the housing crisis by public radio and the local papers.

At most schools it isn't necessary to have a doctorate to be a lecturer. Practitioners with a love for teaching can often pick up a course or two. But if you're looking to make your career in academia, you'll need to invest the extra time and get your PhD, usually three years or more. If you have a love for statistical analysis, in-depth research and a passion for teaching, a career in academia could be the right fit for you.

Lance Freeman

Associate Professor, Urban Planning at Columbia University

Planetizen: What was your career path?

LF: When I was an adolescent, I had an interest in architecture and I stumbled upon the career of city planning as I was investigating college majors.

But in college, I chose what I was advised would be a more pragmatic route as a business manager. I worked for a couple of years in a bank for the local government as a budget analyst in New York City. Eventually, I decided to go back to school to pursue a master's degree in city planning.

I first took a few classes at Hunter College in the evenings, while I was working, to familiarize myself with the field. Then I went back to school full-time at the University of North Carolina Chapel Hill. While I was getting my master's degree I did an internship with the Community Development Corporation in Brooklyn, New York.

While I was in school, I took a civil service exam for the title of city planner in New York City. In New York City we have civil service exams; you take the exam and you pass it. If you pass high enough you will be placed on a list. When a job opening for that title comes open you will be called for an interview.

So I took the exam while I was in graduate school and passed the exam. Just about the time right after I graduated they called me for an interview. I interviewed successfully with the New York City Housing Authority and they hired me to work as a City Planner.

Working for New York City's government,

it was difficult as a planner to really have significant effects at a policy level. It seemed one path would be to go into politics which I didn't want to do or another path, I thought, might be to go into academia where I could actually write about policies.

While I was working there, I became particularly interested in some of the policies related to affordable housing. I wanted to play a bigger role in influencing policy and shaping the policies. That led me to go back to get a PhD at the University of North Carolina Chapel Hill and revive my interest in planning. While I was there I also did some work with community-based organizations, mostly research and technical assistance with community-based organizations throughout North Carolina.

I got a job at a social policy think tank in Washington, D.C., in policy research. I worked there for about a year and a half. Then I taught at the University of Delaware for a year and a half before coming to

Columbia to teach in their Urban Planning Program.

Planetizen: *What are the challenges of working in your position, and what do you like best about working in your position?*

LF: What I like most about my job is that have a lot of freedom to pursue what interests me when it comes to writing and research, I can write and do research on topics that I find interesting. And when I am teaching, I can shape my classes around topics that I think are important and interesting.

I also like the constant interaction with new people who are very excited about the field. Every year, new students are coming into the field, and that's very refreshing. It keeps the job from getting stale.

Sometimes I'm frustrated by the long process between having an idea and when it becomes translated into something that actually happens and has a real effect.

Planetizen: *What advice would you give to someone who is interested in becoming an academic in planning?*

LF: Are you actually curious? Do you like to write? Do you like to communicate your ideas to a broader audience? I think those are some of the things that you need to ask yourself if you are interested in pursuing a career in academia.

And if you are pretty sure that's what you want to do, I think it's very important to find a graduate program that's a good fit for yourself, where there are faculty there who will be able to guide you and have an interest in what you want to pursue. I think that's very important.

Some Significant Universities *(in alphabetical order)*

Cornell University, www.aap.cornell.edu/crp

Harvard University Graduate School of Design, gsd.harvard.edu

Massachussetts Institute of Technology (MIT), http://dusp.mit.edu

Rutgers, the State University of New Jersy, http://policy.rutgers.edu

University of California at Berkeley, dcrp.ced.berkeley.edu

University of California, Los Angeles, www.spa.ucla.edu/main.cfm

University of Illinois at Urbana-Champaign, www.urban.illinois.edu

University of North Carolina at Chapel Hill, www.planning.unc.edu

University of Pennsylvania, www.design.upenn.edu

University of Southern California, www.usc.edu/schools/sppd

Sample Job Description

Job Title: Assistant Professor
Job Type: Planner
Date Posted: 12/17/2008
Organization: Ohio State University
URL: http://knowlton.osu.edu/

The City & Regional Planning section of the Knowlton School of Architecture (KSA) invites applicants for full-time, tenure-track position(s) at the Assistant Professor rank. The start date is Autumn 2009. Reviews will begin on January 26th, 2009 and will continue until the position is filled.

We seek candidates with a strong record or strong promise of scholarship and funded research in one or more of the following areas: urban design and physical planning, sustainable communities, globalism and international development, applications of digital technology, planning law and administration, planning finance and real estate, regional economic planning, social justice, and governance and innovation in both international and domestic contexts. Successful candidates will have both a scholarly and an applied orientation and be well-grounded in the theory and practice of planning in the urban context. They will link a research and teaching agenda to one or more of the section's concentrations: Physical Planning and Design; Environmental and Land Use Planning; International Development Planning; GIS; Housing, Real Estate and Neighborhood Planning; Planning Policy and Process; Transportation Planning; and Urban and Regional Economic Planning. The successful candidates will be able to communicate and work with students from other disciplinary backgrounds including architecture, landscape architecture, science, engineering, social science, and the humanities. A doctorate is required in planning or a related field. Applicants with other terminal degrees may be considered if they have at least a master's degree in planning or can demonstrate significant knowledge of planning.

Located on the main campus of The Ohio State University, the City & Regional Planning section offers a professionally accredited master of city and regional planning degree, along with a research oriented doctoral degree. The program is expanding to include an undergraduate major and the successful candidate will be expected to contribute to all of the academic programs. We have nine faculty members, 110 masters students, 27 PhD students, and actively participate in the School's vibrant learning and research. atmosphere, alongside programs in architecture and landscape architecture.

More Resources

- Association of Collegiate Schools of Planning, www.acsp.org
- The Journal of the American Planning Association, www.planning.org/japa
- The Journal of Planning Education and Research, http://services.bepress.com/jper
- Planners Network, www.plannersnetwork.org

Researcher

The work of urban planning doesn't just happen at city hall. The field is incredibly broad and encompasses jobs and positions that run the gamut from field work to academics. Somewhere in between is the crucial role of the researcher. Researchers and librarians typically do the work and find the information that informs and guides the actual planning on the ground.

Often working for universities or think tanks, researchers are the people who know what information is available and how to find it. They comb through hundreds of new books and reports to locate the most useful and relevant pieces of information to include in future reports, planning documents and articles. There's plenty of work for them to do, and much demand for people who can do that work well.

To be a researcher in the field of planning, it's obviously useful to have a background in urban planning. But like many fields within planning, a defined set of knowledge is not as important as an interest in the field. Reading the literature of the field is a good way to become familiar with the current state of planning and the general direction the research is headed. By following the latest reports and books, one will be better able to understand where the field is moving and what areas of study are taking it there.

Though this detailed knowledge of the field is crucial, most of the work of a librarian or researcher will revolve around simply knowing what information is available and how to organize it to best serve those who need it. Many universities offer education in library science, which teaches various research methods, tools for information organization, statistics, classification and collection management. Libraries are intensely organized, and the librarians and

researchers who operate and use them have to have a similarly intense understanding of that organization.

Applying that knowledge specifically to urban planning is a good way to combine two interests. Being able to aid in the production of research papers and policy analyses will be very attractive talents, depending on the area of involvement in the urban planning realm. Though municipalities often hold a large amount of information, they are not likely to have the resources to keep a librarian on staff. But for organizations in the private sector, like foundations, research groups and public interest groups, the ability to afford researchers is commensurate with the need for their services. Universities are similarly able to keep researchers and librarians on staff.

Michael Dudley (profiled on the next page) is a researcher and librarian at the University of Winnipeg, and he divides his time between running one of the university's libraries, researching and preparing reports for one of its research arms, and assisting students with research and thesis questions. All of this work is based on his ability to find and use information, and his understanding of the materials within the field and within his collection. As he discusses, staying up to date with all the new developments and trends in the field is a major part of his work.

Becoming a librarian may seem like extending graduate school into a job, and in some senses it is. But unlike the majority of graduate school, the work of a researcher has very real impacts in the world. Bright and capable people are needed to do this research and digest this information if planners are going to produce useful and important reports, recommendations and policies.

Michael Dudley

Research Associate and Library Coordinator, Institute of Urban Studies, University of Winnipeg

Planetizen: Describe a typical day at your job.

MD: Well, after deleting 8,000 spam emails, I get on to working on the various reports and research projects that I'm involved with here. We're doing a sustainability plan for a community in northern Manitoba. We were working on a social plan for a community in the south. There are proposals that we work on from time to time, and I often edit reports that other people, other staff members are working on. So, report-writing and editing is a big part of it.

During the academic year, helping students and faculty in the library also becomes a big part of my day. It's not so much an issue over the summer, it's pretty quiet. I also try to fit in blogging and op-eds when I can. We've got a blog here at the Institute of Urban Studies that I've been working on for four years. There are several other blogs that I'm involved with, so my blogging time is spread rather thin.

In addition to my daytime work at the Institute, I'm also a research associate with the Centre for Sustainable Transportation. It is also based here at the University of Winnipeg. So, I do report-writing, editing, and blogging for them, too.

Planetizen: What do you like best about your job?

MD: I like the variety. That it isn't all just one thing. If I had worked for the city I might have been approving development applications and that would be all that I would do, for example. And I know some people who

do that and it kind of gets monotonous. So, I like the variety because I never really know from one week to another what's going on, and the opportunities that I've been given, the conferences the papers. I've done a number of research trips as well for our projects here that have been very interesting. I really like the library work. I really enjoy assisting students and faculty with research on urban topics and in addition to the reference work. The reference work is really nice because we are a small library, we've got a nice intimate setting. And unlike the busy university library across the street where it's pretty frenetic at times, I've got the luxury here with just sitting down with people at the table and saying, "OK, let's talk about your paper topic and let's work out what it is you need."

Planetizen: What would you say is the most challenging part of your job?

MD: Probably the fact that I do have to fit in with projects that I'm not necessarily an expert on. Sometimes the institute will get something and it's like, "OK, I guess I have to do a lot of homework and find out what I can about this topic." But then, of course, at the end of the day you've got this whole new body of knowledge that you didn't have before, which is exciting and you can pass that on and find other applications for it.

And then sometimes, of course, I get students who come in with topics I don't know about. That's very challenging and sometimes I can't help them and have to refer them on. But, there are quite a few libraries in Winnipeg dealing with environmental and urban topics. Basically, the most challenging aspect is that there is so much to know like just keeping up with the state of planning knowledge, current practices and theory, the global context for planning. And, it's just changing so rapidly and the issues are so challenging.

Planetizen: If you were to talk to someone who is interested in following a similar career path, what advice would you offer them?

MD: I tell students interested in both of the fields of planning and librarianship that both are very interdisciplinary, and regardless of what your interests are and what drives you and what your passions are, you can find a place in librarianship or planning because libraries are all about collecting and making accessible the whole range of human experience and history, and planning is all about the city, the built environment, which is also an expression of the human experience through history and our inspirations for the future. So, I think both professions are really inspiring. They both have a lot of potential to make positive change in society.

Some Significant Employers *(in alphabetical order)*

Brookings Institution, www.brookings.edu

Center for Urban Policy Research, Rutgers University, http://policy.rutgers.edu/CUPR

Environmental Design Library, University of California, Berkeley, www.lib.berkeley.edu/ENVI

The Ohio State University, Knowlton School of Architecture Library
http://library.osu.edu/sites/architecture

RAND Corporation, www.rand.org/jobs

The Rockefeller Foundation, www.rockfound.org

San Francisco Planning + Urban Research Association, www.spur.org

University of Washington Built Environment Library, www.lib.washington.edu/be

Sample Job Description

Job Title: Director of Research
Job Type: Researcher
Date Posted: 07/13/2009
Organization: World Business Chicago
URL: www.worldbusinesschicago.com

World Business Chicago is a not-for-profit economic development organization. Our mission is to enhance metropolitan Chicago's reputation as a business location and to assist companies seeking to locate or expand in the area.

WBC has a full-time Director of Research position available immediately. Primary responsibilities include:

- Supervising maintenance and development of economic, demographic, and business indicator databases;
- Supervising the maintenance and development of content for WBC's website, presentations and/or marketing materials;
- Responding to requests for information from companies and/or their intermediaries;
- Responding to requests for information from the Mayor's office, City of Chicago departments, media, civic organizations and other affiliates;
- Developing concept papers and teaming with outside researchers to conduct and manage WBC-sponsored research;
- Reviewing and critiquing third-party studies assessing the Chicago economy/business environment;
- Collaborating with WBC Creative, Marketing & Public Relations staff to craft user-friendly materials showcasing Chicago as a business location (brochures, fact books, etc.); and
- Managing Research department staff of at least one Research Associate and interns as needed throughout the year.

The ideal candidate is a detail-oriented, self-starter with strong analytic, organizational and communication skills; the ability to multi-task; and has excellent overall computer proficiency, including Excel, PowerPoint and GIS. A master's degree in economics, urban planning, public policy or a related field is preferred. Relevant work experience may be considered in combination with a degree in an unrelated field. A minimum of four to five years of relevant work experience is required regardless of educational background.

Willingness to work in a deadline-oriented, fast-paced environment is crucial. The position is paid commensurate with experience.

More Resources

- American Library Association, www.ala.org
- Brookings Institution Metropolitan Policy Program, www.brookings.edu/metro.aspx
- Librarians' Internet Index, http://lii.org
- USC School of Policy, Planning and Development, www.usc.edu/sppd

Journalist

Journalist or communications specialist is probably not one of the most likely jobs a planner will get once out of school.

But much of modern-day planning revolves around communication. The ideas and plans developed by planners are often created in conjunction with public participation sessions and other input that helps to guide the ultimate vision or implementation. Being able to communicate what's being done and how places could change will be a critical tool and job requirement for any planner – be they in the public or private sector.

As far as people focusing specifically on communications, the majority of such jobs will largely be found outside of the planning realm. Communications specialists or firms may be brought into to work with planners on certain project, but for the most part the two worlds are separate. People pursuing this type of job would likely have liberal arts degrees or previous experience in communications. They likely wouldn't have much knowledge of planning issues from the beginning.

On the other hand, knowledge of the field could be a positive attribute for job seekers. Being able not only to understand the complexities of the processes of urban development, but also to communicate them to laypeople can be a very attractive set of skills.

These sorts of positions are likely to be found more in the private or non-profit sectors than in municipal government. Think tanks and advocacy groups often employ people who are trained in communicating ideas. These groups often produce white papers and reports and need to get the word out through someone with an authoritative knowledge of the subject matter.

For example, Anthony Flint, Director of Public Affairs for the Lincoln Institute of Land Policy (profiled next page), spends much of his time connecting press people with new reports or arranging interviews with experts at the institute. He also summarizes reports and translates highly technical material into a form that can be easily understood by people unfamiliar with the often complex subject matter.

In a slightly different area, journalism about urban planning has exploded in recent years, largely due to the Internet and the proliferation of blogs. There are many opportunities to write about urban issues, though most will simply be hobby efforts, focusing on specific planning issues in a given community or neighborhood. That being said, command over the written word can be a useful tool and some publications are willing to pay planners who know how to write intelligently about the work they've done or their own personal thoughts on the field.

A good communications specialist should have the ability to process large amounts of information, digest it and reproduce it in a concise, understandable way. To be effective in this role, a solid understanding of urban planning concepts will be very helpful, though it is not required. Much of those details can be learned on the job.

Ultimately, being effective in this sort of job relies heavily on understanding the role of communication in the planning process and being able to facilitate that communication.

It's not propaganda, nor is it outright advertising. Of course, the circumstances will change depending on the organization and sector, but for the most part, any job in communications related to planning will focus primarily on encouraging conversation, not directing it.

Anthony Flint

Director of Public Affairs, Lincoln Institute of Land Policy

Planetizen: What's a typical day on your job?

AF: I come in here and on a typical day there might be an inquiry from the outside world. And this can be from a reporter who is working on a story, or it could be a chief of staff for a state legislator who is looking for information on circuit breakers for the property tax. It could be someone from the *New York Times.* So I try to – in those cases – line up the journalists with our expertise here, and our sources here. And then I would typically do some work on the website, which is a process where you really just build on your successes and your work. And you just keep building on it and it's a layered thing, because you just can't rest, you always have to be making it better.

Then I might do a blog post. Say, for instance, we have an event or a lecture that's interesting. I would cover it pretty much like I did when I was a reporter at the Boston Globe, but instead of filing a story, I would just file a blog post. If anything, that's been hard to keep up with.

If it's a travel day, I would be at some place like the Congress for New Urbanism or The American Planning Association or New Partners for Smart Growth - perhaps being on a panel, perhaps one of our experts here that's on a panel, presenting the findings of a report, for example. And then occasionally I would actually have a speaking engagement myself related to my books, but also related to the work of the Lincoln Institute, because they tend to go hand-in-hand.

Planetizen: What do you like best about your job?

AF: What's really satisfying is being able to provide a working paper for that staffer in the state legislature on the topic that they are looking for. Or being able to point someone to a report by just saying, "It's right up there on the website, just go to the home page and click on this." That's really what I like best, because like journalism and writing about planning and development, this is on a different, and in some ways a bigger scale contributing to the dialog and promoting a public dialog about these issues which I obviously think are important.

For example, if we are able to help a community with a charrette, or resolve a land use dispute. Or to help a state or local government recast its policies in some way – on the property tax or something else like that. Or, even the most ambitious goal we have now, is to be a source of information and analysis for the Obama administration, particularly in climate and infrastructure issues. Then we really feel like we are having an impact.

Planetizen: What is the most challenging part about your job?

AF: Sometimes it's challenging to build bridges with the more academic and scholarship side of things. Sometimes it's challenging to ask scholars to make more of a firm conclusion and to also translate some of the more technical things accurately.

I'm learning all the time, it's kind of fun, but I'm learning about econometrics and all kinds of other things that I never would have guessed. It brings me back to my Economics 101 class, way back when. It can sometimes be challenging to stay up to speed with some very smart people that I deal with everyday.

Planetizen: You mentioned that you started out in journalism, and you never went to school

for planning per se. You were a Loeb Fellow for a year within the Harvard Graduate School of Design, so you gained some formal education there. How important would you say a basic knowledge in planning is to what you do?

AF: I think it's actually helpful to have the liberal arts education I started out with. A communications background and being able to write, I think, really helps. I'm not sure how important the formal education is. I did mention the Loeb Fellowship, and I do think that, for a lot of reasons, was pretty critical. I needed to look at the history of cities and understand Olmsted and Burnham and Le Corbusier. In that sense, in one way or another, you got to have a general background and an education in planning issues. Some of the technical stuff, I feel, you can kind of learn on the job.

Some Significant Employers *(in alphabetical order)*

Associated Press, www.ap.org

Curbed, curbed.com

Metropolis Magazine, www.metropolismag.com

Next American City, http://americancity.org

Planning Magazine, www.planning.org/planning

Streetsblog, www.streetsblog.org

The New York Times, www.nytimes.com

The Washington Post, www.washingtonpost.com

Sample Job Description

Job Title: Reporter/Blogger
Job Type: Journalist
Date Posted: 03/13/2009
Organization: The Open Planning Project
URL: http://openplans.org

We are the producers of Streetsblog. org and a national network of more than 200 progressive transportation policy bloggers called Streetsblog.net. Since its launch three years ago, Streetsblog has broken numerous stories and emerged as an influential voice in civic affairs in New York and other cities. Our readership consists largely of planning and transportation professionals, environmental advocates, government employees, members of the media and individuals involved in what is often referred to as the "Livable Streets" movement.

With major transportation, climate, and energy legislation coming before Congress in 2009 and 2010, we are seeking a talented journalist to cover Capitol Hill for Streetsblog. We are looking for a reporter/blogger who can help bring outside-the-Beltway readers inside the legislative process, scoop the mainstream press, and make Streetsblog Capitol Hill an engaging and entertaining must-read.

Our ideal candidate is a talented, experienced writer and reporter who knows the players in transportation and environmental policymaking on Capitol Hill. The ability to navigate the intricacies of the legislative process, to dig beneath the surface, and to track the interests and influences behind the scene is a must.

While Streetsblog has a distinct advocacy bent oriented towards reducing automobile dependence and improving conditions for pedestrians, cyclists and transit riders, we bring newspaper-quality journalism to the issues that we cover. Towards that end, we are seeking a reporter/blogger with previous professional experience to do original research, interviews, and coverage of events.

Qualifications include:

* Professional journalism experience, ideally covering the legislative processes related to transportation, planning or environmental policy issues.
* A network of existing sources – and an ability to cultivate new sources – among the lawmakers, lobbyists, advocates and other players who work on federal transportation policy issues.
* Experience with WordPress or other blogging technologies is a plus.
* A personal passion for the issues that Streetsblog covers.

More Resources

* American Journalism Review, www.ajr.org
* Columbia Journalism Review, www.cjr.org
* Poynter Institute for Media Studies, www.poynter.org
* Society of Professional Journalists, www.spj.org

Representative Jobs

Salary information can be difficult to come by. Except for government jobs, salary ranges are rarely included in public job listings. But before you begin working towards a career, it's certainly useful to understand what you might be able to make.

Over the next three pages, you'll find a detailed list of several actual job listings we found over the 2008-2009 period that include details on salary. Rather than find a statistical average salary for each career, we decided it would be more useful to see a number of jobs from different regions and at different levels of experience to give you a taste of the variety of pay grades. We've included three jobs for every career included in this guide, and an extra three for city planner to reflect the variety of pay grades

from Planner 1 to Planning Director.

The numbers are revealing. Planning commissioners are rarely paid much, and sometimes not at all. Positions in the southern and central U.S. pay about 25% less than jobs on the coasts. And academic jobs pay better than one might have expected.

Of course, this is just an abbreviated, random sampling. For more thorough data, consult the Bureau of Labor Statistics (www.bls.gov) or the American Planning Association's 2008 Planners Salary Survey (www.planning.org/salary).

And for up-to-date job listings, subscribe to Planetizen's weekly Jobswire newsletter, delivering the latest twenty job listings directly to your email box at no charge (www.planetizen.com/jobswire/subscribe).

Representative Jobs

Table 1: Planning

Job Title	Location	Low	High	Experience
City Planner II	Baton Rouge, LA	$34,820	$34,820	1-3 years
Planner I/II	Visalia, CA	$42,816	$58,272	4-6 years
City Planner II	Valdosta, GA	$35,000	$50,000	4-6 years
City Planner II	Fairbanks, AK	$46,758	$46,758	1-3 years
City Planner	Rosemead, CA	$93,863	$113,397	7-10 years
City Planner	Leavenworth, KS	$50,760	$63,450	4-6 years
Principal Planner	Courtland, VA	$48,612	$48,612	4-6 years
5928 Planner III	San Francisco, CA	$79,066	$96,096	4-6 years
Town Planner	Truckee, CA	$83,604	$112,872	4-6 years
Planner or Sr. Planner	Lincoln City, OR	$44,868	$57,288	4-6 years
Planner	Aberdeen, SD	$39,732	$39,732	4-6 years
Senior Planner	Beaufort, SC	$40,000	$45,000	4-6 years
Senior Planner	San Francisco, CA	$93,938	$114,166	7-10 years
Senior Planner	State College, PA	$51,207	$55,983	4-6 years
Planning Director	Augusta, GA	$50,000	$60,000	4-6 years
Director, Land Use & Growth Management	Leonardtown, MD	$100,000	$120,000	7-10 years
Deputy Director - Building Permits & Inspections	El Paso, TX	$84,821	$139,954	7-10 years
Regional Planner/ Associate Regional Planner	Stockton, CA	$58,200	$78,600	1-3 years
Regional Planner	Anniston, AL	$37,520	$37,520	1-3 years
Regional Growth Coordinator	Manhattan, KS	$45,323	$49,855	1-3 years
Community Planner, Navy	Okinawa, Japan	$40,093	$91,801	1-3 years
Community Planner, Army Corps	Washington, DC	$96,459	$160,860	not specified
Community Planner, NAVFAC	Ft. Worth, TX	$40,093	$91,801	1-3 years
Planner/Zoning Administrator	Marshfield, WI	$48,746	$57,763	1-3 years
Zoning Administrator	Alachua County, FL	$57,106	$94,225	4-6 years
Zoning Manager	Mohave County, AZ	$59,862	$92,914	4-6 years
Senior Environmental Planner	San Francisco, CA	$80,047	$97,298	4-6 years
Commissioner of Planning & Environmental Management	Monticello, NY	$75,000	$85,000	4-6 years
Air Quality Program Manager	Kansas City, MO	$54,350	$62,000	4-6 years
Strategic Planner for Public Health	Fairfax, VA	$69,106	$92,141	4-6 years
Public Health Planner	Arlington, VA	$53,040	$87,672	4-6 years

Table 1: Planning *(continued)*

Job Title	Location	Low	High	Experience
Public Health Administrator	Tallahassee, FL	$33,057	$144,326	All levels
Project Manager, Strategic Planning	Wellington, FL	$51,181	$81,271	4-6 years
Planning Consultant	Stillwater, MN	$53,019	$72,613	4-6 years
Principal Planner	Washington, DC	$110,000	$160,000	10+ years
National & State Register Historian	Denver, CO	$36,900	$41,040	1-3 years
State Historic Preservation Officer	Santa Fe, NM	$67,500	$84,500	4-6 years
Historic Preservationist	Richmond, VA	$40,959	$52,981	4-6 years
GIS Administrator	Merced, CA	$48,492	$59,496	7-10 yrs
GIS Administrator	Auburn, AL	$34,954	$44,977	1-3 years
GIS Administrator	Aiken, SC	$45,000	$45,000	4-6 years
Real Estate Attorney	Long Island, NY	$100,000	$100,000	7-10 years
Land Use Lawyer/Law Fellow	New York, NY	$55,000	$60,000	1-3 years
Land Use Attorney	San Diego, CA	$94,940	$94,940	4-6 years

Table 2: Design

Job Title	Location	Low	High	Experience
Urban Planner/ Designer	Buena Park, CA	$49,962	$63,378	1-3 years
Urban Designer	Waterstown, MA	$65,000	$65,000	4-6 years
Urban Designer	New York, NY	$62,000	$62,000	1-3 years
Landscape Architect	Washington, DC	$49,314	$112,915	4-6 years
Landscape Architect	U.S. Forest Service	$53,234	$79,781	4-6 years
Landscape Architect	Tuscon, AZ	$34,000	$37,000	4-6 years
Architect - Project Manager	Scranton, PA	$62,132	$100,976	4-6 years
Senior Architect/CADD Operator	Carle Place, NY	$40,000	$80,000	4-6 years
Architect	Los Angeles, CA	$65,000	$75,000	4-6 years

Representative Jobs

Table 3: Development

Job Title	Location	Low	High	Experience
Community Development Administrator	Westminster, CO	$62,664	$87,732	4-6 years
Real Estate Development Program Manager	Des Moines, IA	$45,000	$60,000	4-6 years
Project Manager - Real Estate Development	Philadelphia, PA	$59,000	$74,000	4-6 years
Manager of Planning & Development	Lac la Biche, Alberta, Canada	$76,892	$92,865	7-10 years
CDA Redevelopment Project Manager	Madison, WI	$62,073	$74,938	1-3 years
Senior Project Manager (Replacement Housing)	Bridgeport, CT	$58,000	$73,000	4-6 years
Economic Development Coordinator	Ocala, FL	$45,885	$73,050	4-6 years
M2-Economic Development	Rockville, MD	$73,811	$133,992	7-10 years
Director of Planning and Development Services	Everett, WA	$122,556	$149,324	7-10 years

Table 4: Transport

Job Title	Location	Low	High	Experience
Transportation Planner	Pittsfield, MA	$55,000	$70,000	4-6 years
Principal Transportation Planner	Portland, OR	$64,314	$86,086	1-3 years
Transportation Planning Manager	Wichita, KS	$61,722	$111,976	4-6 years
Regional Multi-Modal Planning Director	Fort Collins, CO	$59,200	$88,800	4-6 years
Airport Planner II	San Diego, CA	$52,650	$68,442	4-6 years
Principal Airport Planner	Dallas, TX	$86,000	$86,000	10+ years
Airport Planner	Cincinnati, OH	$80,000	$150,000	10+ years

Table 5: Politics

Job Title	Location	Low	High	Experience
Policy Advisor	New York, NY	$70,000	$90,000	4-6 years
Program/Policy Anlayst, Bicycle and Pedestrian Coordinator	Madison, WI	$34,598	$57,088	1-3 years
Policy Director	Oakland, CA	$70,000	$85,000	7-10 years
Planning Commissioner	Macob, MI	$2,174	$2,174	none
Planning Commissioner	Bothell, WA	$6,000	$6,000	none
Planning Commissioner	Portland, OR	none	none	none
City Councilmember	Austin, TX	$57,736	$57,736	not specified
Mayor	Bremerton, WA	$118,000	$118,000	not specified
City Councilmember	San Jose, CA	$86,625	$86,625	not specified

Table 6: Research

Job Title	Location	Low	High	Experience
GIS Certificate Coordinator	Baltimore, MD	$60,000	$60,000	1-3 years
Adjunct Professor - Urban Planning	Los Angeles, CA	$66,100	$83,700	4-6 years
Landscape Architecture/Planning Professor	Manhattan, KS	$77,800	$11,833	7-10 years
Researcher - Post-doctoral Research Associate	Lincoln, NE	$50,000	$50,000	4-6 years
Researcher - Researcher	New York, NY	$40,000	$55,000	1-3 years
Researcher - Research Associate	Oakland, CA	$45,000	$50,000	1-3 years
City/Politics Reporter	Loveland, CO	$25,000	$30,000	1-3 years
Government Reporter	Hamilton, MO	$20,000	$25,000	1-3 years
Manager of Communications	Arlington, VA	$60,000	$75,000	4-6 years

Acknowledgements

The editors would like to first thank all of the professionals we interviewed for their generous participation. The world of planning is fascinatingly varied, and it was a treat to get this insider's look into their work.

Thanks to Richard Florida and Paul Smoke for their insightful essays.

Thanks also to our own Cate Miller for her tireless assistance, Josh Stephens for his meticulous copyediting, and interns Alek Miller and Liyuan Huang for doggedly gathering data on job descriptions and salary ranges.

The Planetizen Team

Editors-in-Chief/Founders: Chris Steins & Abhijeet Chavan
Managing Editor: Tim Halbur
Assistant Editor: Nate Berg
Art Director: Mindy Oliver
Operations Manager: Cate Miller
Lead Developer: Ki Kim

Made in the USA
Charleston, SC
20 August 2013